COMPANY OF ONE

Company
of
ONE

WHY STAYING SMALL IS THE NEXT
BIG THING FOR BUSINESS

Paul Jarvis

Houghton Mifflin Harcourt

Boston   New York

2019

For information about permission to reproduce selections
from this book, write to trade.permissions@hmhco.com or to
Permissions, Houghton Mifflin Harcourt Publishing Company,
3 Park Avenue, 19th Floor, New York, New York 10016.

hmhco.com

Library of Congress Cataloging-in-Publication Data
Names: Jarvis, Paul (Business writer), author.
Title: Company of one : why staying small is the next big thing for business
/ Paul Jarvis.
Description: Boston : Houghton Mifflin Harcourt, [2019] |
Includes bibliographical references and index.
Identifiers: LCCN 2017061483 (print) | LCCN 2018001193 (ebook) |
ISBN 9781328972378 (ebook) | ISBN 9781328972354 (hardcover)
Subjects: LCSH: Small business. | Strategic planning.
Classification: LCC HD2341 (ebook) | LCC HD2341 .J37 2019 (print) |
DDC 658.02/2—dc23
LC record available at https://lccn.loc.gov/2017061483

Book design by Chrissy Kurpeski

Printed in the United States of America
DOC 10 9 8 7 6 5 4 3 2 1

For Luna

There's no such thing as perpetual growth. Yet that's what traditional business people crave. But what is growth meant to achieve? If Oxford University is so successful, then why isn't there a branch in Washington, D.C.? If a symphony is successful with 120 musicians, why not even more so with 600? "To grow bigger" is not much of an effective business strategy at all.

— RICARDO SEMLER, CEO OF SEMCO PARTNERS

Contents

Prologue

On February 28, 2010 — the final day of the Winter Olympics in Vancouver — I found myself driving a tiny cube-van with my wife, Lisa, heading to a ferry terminal. We had just closed on the sale of our condo, a small glass box in the sky located right in the heart of downtown Vancouver. We had also sold or donated almost all of our possessions, and we were moving to a town in the middle of nowhere, literally at the end of the road on Vancouver Island.

Our new town — Tofino — was proudly billed as "life on the edge." As in truly the edge of nowhere. This island is the setting for the reality TV show *Alone*, where the actors grapple with living and surviving in complete isolation; it's filmed a few hours north of town. Fewer than 2,000 people live in Tofino — mostly surfers, old draft dodgers, and other assorted hippies who are still very happy living in the twentieth century.

At the time — before, after, and even during the move — I was working entirely online as a designer and online business consultant to everyone from Mercedes-Benz to Microsoft to Marie Forleo. My work and life depended on being hyperconnected. But now I was trading all of that for a town with zero other people involved in tech and, even worse, a really awful internet connection.

In short, for someone like myself who was coming from the

tech world, this move was going to be a *bit* of a massive adjustment.

The main reason I was hell-bent on leaving civilization was
that I had simply had enough of "business as usual" city life and
the constant push from others to grow my successful business
into something bigger. My wife, Lisa, too, was sick of her daily career demands. We were both done with the constant stimulus and
stress of our urban existence — the lights, sounds, and distractions, the constant and incessant "buzzing." To save our sanity,
we made our escape as quickly as we possibly could. And living on
Vancouver Island seemed like the perfect tonic.

Yet we soon learned that living in the woods on an island does
something funny — it forces you to go deep within your own
thoughts. There's not a whole lot else you can do, especially if you
don't have a television or even Netflix. And at first, exploring your
own thoughts is one of the scariest things in the world. (A study
at the University of Virginia by Timothy Wilson found that people would rather get electric shocks than simply be alone with
their thoughts.) But then again, if you sit with your thoughts for a
while, they can reveal some mind-set-changing ideas.

But scaling down wasn't just a plan for getting rid of our physical belongings; it was also a plan for achieving mental clarity. In
creating a personal life that was bare of all but the essentials, par-
allels to my work started to become evident — what was truly necessary and what wasn't. By decluttering my thoughts (creating
an "inbox zero" for my brain, if you will), I was able to look at my
day-to-day business much more clearly because the distractions
were now gone. I hadn't been able to clearly express my reasons
for the way I had been working until that moment.

This clarity highlighted something I had unconsciously been
doing for nearly twenty years, even before going out on my own,
and that was building a business full of resilience, driven by a desire for autonomy and, on most days, enjoyment. In other words,

by scaling down every aspect of my life, I realized this was how I had successfully built my business all along. I had benefited immensely by resisting the typical avenues of growth and business expansion. (Hey, I was able to move to the woods on an island.) And now, for the very first time, I understood why.

I had been building a company of one.

INTRODUCING A COMPANY OF ONE

At first, I felt alone in my assumption that more isn't always better. But then, during the writing of this book, I found that there is an amassing army of others who feel very much the same, and whose business decisions are backed up with growing research and studies. It turns out that some of the most successful brand-name companies and individuals are companies of one at heart.

Living in Tofino gave me the opportunity to take up a daily ritual of going for a morning surf. One day I was out in the lineup (the place just in front of the breaking waves where surfers wait to catch rides) with my accountant friend. We were sitting out there, waiting for the next decent wave, and he turned to me and said, "I'm stoked! I've just about made enough to take the rest of the year off to go rock climbing." It was August. Puzzled by what he said, I missed the next few waves that rolled by. Once he paddled back to the lineup, where I still was, he explained that he had calculated what he needed to make in profit in order to cover his cost of living and put a decent amount of money into investments. He had figured out the amount of wealth he needed to be comfortable and didn't feel the need to accumulate more.

Past that, he didn't need any more money — so he'd stop working when he hit his "enough" amount and travel for the rest of the year. He didn't want to grow his accounting business into a bigger company with employees and offices in every city. If he did, his "enough" number would also grow, from having to manage more employees and a bigger business. He wouldn't be able to spend as much time rock climbing (or surfing). His focus in his business was being better, not growing bigger. I quickly began to realize that I had adopted a similar mind-set: I knew what I needed to make to cover my business and my life, so I could decide to slow down when I reached "enough" as well.

It's assumed that hard work and smart thinking always result in business growth. But the opposite is often true: not all growth is beneficial, and some growth can actually reduce your resilience and your autonomy. Just as I learned new skills in self-sufficiency that were far outside my realm of knowledge, companies of one can do the same. Indeed, they'll need to in order to stand out and thrive.

In truth, embracing growth appears to be the easier route more often than not, since it's easier to throw "more" at any problem that might pop up. Want more customers? *Hire more employees.* Need more revenue? *Spend more.* Fielding more support requests? *Build a bigger support team.* But scaling up might not be the best or smartest solution to the basic problem. As a means to generating higher profits, what if you acquired more customers simply by creating more efficiency, so you didn't have to hire more people? What if you generated more revenue by finding a way to spend less (again, for higher profits)? What if you responded to the growth in support requests by finding a better way to teach your customers how to use what you sell, so they didn't have to ask questions as often? What if you didn't have to work more hours to finish a project but just more efficiently, so you could then enjoy more of your life away from work?

Growth, in the typical business sense, isn't always a smart strategy if it's followed blindly. Much of the research reported in this book will strongly suggest that blind growth is the main cause of business problems. It can leave you with an unmaintainable number of employees, unsustainable costs, and more work than hours in a day. It can force you to lay off employees, sell your company at a less than optimal price, or, even worse, close up shop completely.

What if you worked instead toward growing smaller, smarter, more efficient, and more resilient?

Staying small doesn't have to be a stepping-stone to something else, or the result of a business failure — rather, it can be an end goal or a smart long-term strategy. The point of being a company of one is to become better in ways that don't incur the typical setbacks of growth. You can scale up revenue, enjoyment, raving fans, focus, autonomy, and experiences while resisting the urge to blindly scale up employee payroll, expenses, and stress levels. This approach builds both a profit buffer for your company to weather markets and a personal buffer to help you thrive even in times of hardship.

The "company of one" approach doesn't apply only to a single-person business — it's a model for using the power of you to be more self-reliant and more responsible for your own career path. Although a company of one can certainly be a small or single-person business, it's unlike most small businesses, whose end game is usually expansion or growth to hit peak profitability. A company of one questions growth and stays small on purpose.

A company of one isn't simply a practicing freelancer either. While freelancing is a perfect first step to becoming a company of one, freelancers are different because they exchange time for money. Whether they're getting paid by the hour or by deliverables, if they're not working, they're not getting paid. All of a freelancer's relationships are one-to-one, meaning that each time paid work occurs, a freelancer has to do something and use his or her time.

In contrast, a company of one is more in line with the traditional definition of an entrepreneur. If you're utilizing systems, automations, and processes to build a long-term business, you're not trading time for money, but instead operating and profiting outside of the time you spend working and beyond your one-to-one relationships. For example, whether you're creating physical products, selling software, or teaching online courses, customers and users can purchase and consume these products and services without your company of one putting in time for each transaction. While developing products can be time-consuming and iterative, the number of customers can be almost infinite for a company of one, and profit then happens outside of time spent. Where a company of one is concerned, as we'll see in coming chapters, scaling customers and even profit doesn't always require scaling employees or resources exponentially.

A company of one is a collective mind-set and model that can be used by anyone, from a small business owner to a corporate leader, to take ownership and responsibility for what they do to become a valuable asset in any marketplace — in terms of both mental practices and business applications. It's a blueprint for growing a lean and agile business that can survive every type of economic climate, and ultimately it leads to a richer and more meaningful life — no cable-cutting or moving to the woods on an island required.

Just as Michael Pollan's food ideology is summarized in three simple rules — "eat food, not too much, mostly plants" — the "company of one" model can be laid out in a similar fashion: "start small, define growth, and keep learning."

COMPANY OF ONE

PART I

Begin

1

Defining a Company of One

I N THE FALL OF 2010, Tom Fishburne quit his seemingly great career as the vice president of marketing at a large consumer foods company. He wanted to draw cartoons. This turned out to be Tom's best career move — both emotionally and, surprisingly, financially.

He wasn't just following his passion on a whim, nor did he become some sort of anti-capitalist hippie. He carefully planned out and executed his decision to ensure, as much as anyone could, that he would thrive.

As a child, Tom was obsessed with drawing cartoons — so much so that he would take his doctor father's prescription pad and draw flip-books on the back.

Then, at Harvard, while working toward his MBA, his friends prompted him to submit cartoons to the campus paper, the *Harbus,* which he did for the rest of the time he was at school. Still, once finished with school, he took a job in the corporate world, because it seemed like the logical next step after receiving a business degree. Tom was also part of the SITCOM demographic (Single Income Two Children Oppressive Mortgage), so he figured he needed a "stable" job. Cartooning remained a hobby, however, and he would share with coworkers his cartoons poking fun at corporate marketing — the very industry he was now part of.

As Tom worked his corporate job and his cartoons were shared by his friends, and then by their friends, and then outside their circle, they started to garner attention. He began taking on side jobs to draw during the evenings and weekends for companies that were eager to pay him. It wasn't until he had a safe runway of such clients lined up, and money saved up, that he pulled the trigger to leave his corporate career and start his own venture.

In the seven years since quitting, Tom has made two to three times more income as a cartoonist than when he was an executive. This didn't happen because he grew an agency, or hired more employees, or expanded to having satellite offices around the globe. His company, Marketoon, is still just he and his wife, along with a few freelancers who work only on isolated projects. Tom and his wife work from home, in a sunny studio in their backyard in Marin County, California, where their two daughters regularly sit and draw cartoons in the afternoon with them.

Traditionally in business, growth has always been seen as a byproduct of success. But Tom doesn't care much for how things are supposed to work. He knows the rules of business — he studied at one of the top schools in the world, then put that knowledge to work at a massive corporation. He just wasn't interested in following those conventional rules.

Typically, when a company does well, it hires more people, builds more infrastructure, and works at increasing its bottom line. There's a core assumption that growth is always good, is always unlimited, and is required for success. Anything else is pushed aside as not being a top priority. If Tom had grown his company, even though he has a waiting list of clients wanting to hire him, he'd have less time to draw cartoons (as he'd be too busy managing cartoonists) and would have far less time with his family in their backyard studio. For Tom, that kind of growth wouldn't be smart or logical. It would go against what he values in his life and in his career.

Consumer culture says the same thing—that more is always better. Through advertising, we're sold a bill of goods that requires us to love the things we buy only until a newer or bigger version is put out for sale. Bigger houses, faster cars, more stuff to pack into our closets, garages, and then, inevitably, our storage lockers. But under this hype, this fetishization of wanting more, are empty promises of happiness and fulfillment that never seem to come to fruition. Sometimes "enough" or even less is all we need, since "more" too often equates to more stress, more problems, and more responsibilities in both life and business.

We can easily run a business with less, although to many people that seems counterintuitive. Tom doesn't have to worry about human resources, rent for office space, salaries, or even the responsibility of managing employees. He hires outside people only when a paying project requires them, and they too have other clients and other work; they can fend for themselves when they're not working on a job for Marketoon.

Tom has been able to create a stable, long-term business that's small enough to handle any economic climate, resilient enough to not have to lean too heavily on a single project or client, and autonomous enough to let him build a life around his work (not the other way around). He's been able to grow his revenue without having to also grow the trappings that typically come with it. He's a brilliant businessperson who gets to spend every day with his family, drawing cartoons, with his daughters, for multinational companies that pay him much more than most illustrators earn.

In short, Tom is the perfect example of a company of one.

A COMPANY OF ONE, DEFINED

A company of one is simply a business that *questions* growth.

A company of one resists and questions some forms of traditional growth, not on principle, but because growth isn't always the most beneficial or financially viable move. It can be a small business owner or a small group of founders. Employees, executive leaders, board members, and corporate leaders who want to work with more autonomy and self-sufficiency can adopt the principles of a company of one as well. In fact, if big businesses want to keep their brightest minds in their employ, they should look to adopt some of the principles of companies of one.

I've personally seen the most success in my life when I've figured out solutions to problems without having to do what traditional businesses do to solve problems — hire more people, throw more money at the problem, or build complex infrastructures to support the extra employees. Basically, I'm not interested in addressing problems by throwing "more" at them. Solving with "more" means more complexity, more costs, more responsibilities, and typically more expenses. More is generally the easiest answer, but not the smartest. I've found both delight and financial benefits in working out solutions to problems without growing. Instead, I and many others enjoy handling problems with the resources currently available. Although it can require a little more ingenuity, solving problems this way can set a business up for long-term stability, since less is needed to keep it afloat.

In October 2016, I wrote a blog post saying I wasn't interested in exponentially growing any company I own or build. I felt like the single red fish in a school of green ones. But then an interesting thing happened: replies started to pour in. People doing all sorts of exciting things in business, from selling fair-trade caramels to working at the biggest tech companies to manufacturing clothing, emailed me that they felt the same way—they had resisted traditional growth and had benefited from it. As I started to develop my own ideas around this concept of staying small and questioning growth, I continued to discover more and more research, stories, and examples of others doing the same. I found that there's a silent movement to approach business in this way that isn't just for cash-strapped tech startups or people who make just enough to scrape by. This movement includes individuals and businesses making six and seven figures and becoming happier than most businesspeople are with the work they do. The school of red fish is, ironically enough, growing.

THE RISE OF COMPANIES OF ONE

Technically, everyone should be a company of one.

Even at a large corporation, you're essentially the only person who looks out for your own best interests and continued employment. No one else cares about you keeping your job as much as you do. It's your responsibility to define and achieve your own success, even in a larger framework of employment.

It can be harder to be a company of one within a corporation, but it's not impossible. Companies of one within organizations can thrive and even be responsible for massive progress. Over the years these individuals have been credited with everything from inventing Post-it notes to developing Sony's PlayStation.

The word "intrapreneur" points to one example of a company of one within a larger organization. It describes corporate leaders who come up with their own goals and then execute them. They don't need much direction, micromanaging, or oversight, as they've been given full work autonomy. They know what needs doing and they just do it. They're aware of the needs of the company and how their talents fit, and they just get to work.

Where the term "intrapreneur" varies from a company of one is that intrapreneurs are typically responsible for product creation and marketing — that is, creating something new, with the resources of the company behind them. Companies of one within organizations don't need to be managers or create products — they simply need to find suitable ways to become better and more productive, without more resources or team members. They can certainly be managers or product creators, but that's not the only definition.

Companies of one within larger corporations have a history of helping large corporations make breakthroughs and dominate markets. Dave Myers, who worked for W. L. Gore and Associates, the company that makes GoreTex fabric, was given "dabble" time to develop new ideas within the company and ultimately came up with the idea to use a kind of coating they were already manufacturing on guitar strings. The result was the best-selling acoustic guitar string brand, Elixir (the strings I use on my guitars — they're head and shoulders above the competition). Sometimes companies of one happen by accident. Dr. Spencer Silver, a scientist at 3M, was working to create an adhesive for aerospace. In playing with the formula, he created a lighter adhesive that didn't leave any residue. It wouldn't work for planes, but it was perfect for paper products, and thus Post-it notes were born.

Some large corporations, like Google, give their employees "personal time" to experiment with ideas outside their typical job roles. Facebook uses "hackathons," which typically last several days and bring together computer programmers to collaborate on something big in a relatively short amount of time. It was a hackathon that led to the creation of Facebook's "Like" button, which arguably connects its ecosystem to the rest of the internet.

In a recent study, Vijay Govindarajan, a professor at Dartmouth, found that for every 5,000 employees, at least 250 will be true innovators and 25 will be innovators and great intrapreneurs (or companies of one) as well.

Many large corporations have companies of one hiding within them. If the skills and passion for innovation and autonomy of these employees are fostered, it can greatly benefit the entire business as a whole. But if they are stifled in their creativeness and freethinking, they tend to move on quickly to other employment or entrepreneurialism. They're rarely motivated solely by money or salaries and lean more toward reinventing their job and role in a way that works best for them.

If you're a company of one, your mind-set is to build your business around *your* life, not the other way around. For me, being a company of one means not having to bother with infinite growth, since that was never the purpose of my working. Instead, I just focus on maximizing work in a way that works for me, which can sometimes mean doing less. Work can be done at a pace that suits my sanity rather than one that supports costly overhead, expenses, or salaries. As much as I enjoy growing my wealth, I also realize that there's a point of diminishing returns if I don't also take care of myself and my well-being.

Society has ingrained in us a very particular idea of what success in business looks like. You work as many hours as possible, and when your business starts to do well, you scale everything up in every direction. To this day, this strategy is considered what it takes to be a success in business — solving problems by adding "more" to the solution. Anyone who stays small, in this line of thinking, hasn't done well enough to add "more" to the mix. But what if we challenge this way of thinking in business? What if staying small is what a company does when it's figured out how to solve problems without adding "more" to them?

Growth, especially blind growth, isn't the best solution to any problem a business might face. And going further, growing your business might actually be the worst decision you could make for the longevity of your business.

So a company of one is not anti-growth, or anti-revenue, and it's not just a one-person business either (although it certainly can be). It's also not just working with a tech-focused or startup mind-set, although leaning on technology, automation, and the connectedness of the internet definitely makes it easier to be a company of one. A company of one questions growth first, and then resists it if there's a better, smarter way forward.

Next, let's look at the four typical traits of all companies of one: resilience, autonomy, speed, and simplicity.

Resilience

Danielle LaPorte, a best-selling author and self-made entrepreneur, reaches millions of people each month with her message of conscious goal-setting and entrepreneurship and is one of Oprah's (yes, *that* Oprah) "Super Soul 100" leaders. But in the beginning, she was fired by the very CEO she had hired months earlier.

In believing that exponential growth was required for her business (more on this in Chapter 2), she took $400,000 in funding from private investors with the provision that she had to hire a *"wunderkind* CEO" to run the business. So she incorporated and hired a thought-to-be superstar.

But six months later, the investors and CEO wanted to change the business model, which meant relegating Danielle's role to just a few blog posts a month and substantially decreasing her pay. Note: named after her, the business was a personality-driven brand based on her own unique personality and style.

Once Danielle got over the supreme shock of what happened, which involved a lot of yoga, tears, and good friends, she began to bounce back. She brought on a new team of A-players, created a website within a few weeks, and figured out the fastest way to start making money on her own with a new business that she had full control over. She began offering consulting services that became so popular that she had to create a waiting list, and then she wrote a best-selling book.

In all the success of her new website, she realized that the strings attached to other people's money are often those other people's opinions about your business and your life. In hardship, she was able to find her path to becoming a company of one. Being or becoming a company of one has a lot to do with resilience: the capacity and fortitude to recover quickly from difficulties — like a changing job market, or being fired. Like a shift in a larger company's focus, or the need to adapt to new disruptive technology — or even to avoid being replaced by robots. (No, this book isn't a taking a turn toward sci-fi . . . more on this in a second.)

Dean Becker, the CEO of Adaptiv Learning Systems, has been researching and developing programs around the idea of resilience since 1997. His company found that the level of resilience a person exhibits determines their success in business, far more than their level of education, training, or experience. Contrary to popular belief, resilience isn't something that only a select few are born with. It can most definitely be learned. Resilient people possess three — absolutely learnable — characteristics.

The first trait that resilient people have is *an acceptance of reality*. They don't need for things to be a certain way and don't engage in wishful thinking. Instead of imagining "if only this changed, I could thrive," they have a down-to-earth view that most of what happens in our lives is not entirely within our control and the best we can do is to steer the boat a little as we float down the river of life. For example, I'm not going to stop writing today because my neighbor is using his deafening chainsaw. Rather, I'm just going to close my window, turn on some electronic music, and get back to work. Danielle LaPorte didn't throw in the towel after being fired; instead, she took a minute, regrouped, then started again.

Often, it's easier to accept reality with a bit of dark humor. My wife, a firefighter and first responder, regularly jokes around with her department because they're routinely exposed to the worst day of someone's life — houses burning down, heart attacks, even chainsaw accidents. Their humor is a way of coping that her fire chief actively encourages, not to make light of bad situations, but to *add* a sense of light to bad situations. Their sense of humor is just as important as their ability to save lives and put out fires. However crass it might sound to an outsider, dark humor helps first responders and firefighters accept their reality and therefore keeps them resilient in doing their essential work.

The second characteristic of resilient people is a sense of *purpose* — being motivated by a sense of meaning rather than by just money. Although purpose and money are not mutually exclusive, you're more likely to be resilient when you know that even in awful or stressful situations, you're working toward a greater and larger good. This sense of purpose comes from values that are unchangeable and central to both individuals and companies as a whole. Companies of one know that they can enjoy their work without always enjoying every aspect of it. So, even if work is sometimes stressful, as long as it relates to a greater whole or a greater end result, that tough work is worth it in the end. For example, you may get stressed out on the day you launch a new product or land a new client, but if the product or the client aligns with the purpose of your business, that momentary anxiety is worth it, since not every day will be nearly as stressful.

The last trait of resilient people in a company of one is *the ability to adapt* when things change — because they invariably do. In Canada, 42 percent of jobs are at risk, according to Ryerson University, from advances in automation, and 62 percent of jobs in America will be in danger within the next ten to twenty years, according to the White House's Council of Economic Advisers in 2016. As much as we can joke about "welcoming our robot overlords" (a memorable quote from the 1977 film adaptation of H. G. Wells's short story "Empire of the Ants"), the threat is real. McDonald's has a robot that can flip a burger in ten seconds and could replace an entire crew within a few years. Tesla and other companies are working on self-driving big rigs to replace truckers for long-range cargo delivery. Highly skilled jobs are also at risk: IBM's Watson, for instance, can suggest available treatments for specific ailments, drawing on the body of medical research and data on disease.

However, what's difficult to automate is exactly what makes a company of one great: the ability to creatively solve problems in new and unique ways without throwing "more" at the problem. Whereas workers in "doing" roles can be replaced by robots or even by other workers, the role of creatively solving difficult problems is more dependent on an irreplaceable individual. Regardless of the rise of the so-called robot overlords, this is where the strength of a company of one lies.

A company of one sees coming shifts like the above and can pivot. For example, an interior designer may spend less time measuring and ordering supplies and more time creating innovative design concepts based on a unique client's needs. Or a financial adviser may spend less time analyzing a client's financial situation and more time understanding the client's particular needs and teaching them how best to manage their money.

These industry disruptions or market changes aren't a sky-is-falling scenario — they're truly just opportunities to redefine work and adapt to changes. When I was doing web design full-time, each time an economic bubble burst or a recession hit I found myself in a great place to find more jobs because I could offer the quality of work a larger agency could provide, but at a price that had one less zero in it. And not only was I still making more profit than if I had been salaried at an agency, but I could still make the most of the price I was charging because my overhead was almost nothing past having a computer and writing off the second bedroom in a rented condo. And then, when the economy picked back up, agencies were so busy that they had to farm out work, which I was available for. So either way, I had a model for revenue that larger agencies couldn't have replicated without scaling down immensely.

Improvising when change happens or when difficulties arise in the market allows you to make do with what's at hand, without having to add "more" into the mix — as in, more employees, more expenses, or more infrastructure.

These traits for resilience are absolutely learnable, not just inherent. In fact, they must be learned, and then fostered, if you are creating a company of one.

Autonomy and Control

Companies of one are becoming more popular because people want more control and autonomy in their lives, especially when it comes to their careers. This is why so many people are choosing this path: being a company of one lets you control your own life and your job.

But to achieve autonomy as a company of one, you have to be a master at your core skill set. Competence and autonomy are tied together because the opposite — having complete control but not a clue what you're doing — is a recipe for disaster. So just as Tom commanded a knowledge of marketing from his Harvard MBA education and subsequent corporate marketing job, as well as a talent for drawing that he had fostered since childhood and worked at weekly, you have to have a skill set, or a combination of skills, that's in demand. With a well-developed skill set, you'll know what areas will benefit from growth and what potential places for growth don't make sense.

Basically, you have to be good at your skill set before you can expect to achieve autonomy from using it.

Typically, you can't acquire this mastery without putting in some time at the beginning of your career in a job that's less autonomous, offers less control, and requires less resilience, since you're managed by the whims of someone higher up. Companies of one know how to break standard rules for the greater good. Doing so is tricky, however, as it involves learning the rules first. In the beginning, a pre–company of one adopts the mind-set of a sponge — basically, you learn everything you can about your profession, your industry, and your customers, and you work at collecting valuable skills of your trade.

Corporations that excel at creating autonomy for their best employees often empower them to become something like companies of one: these employees work faster and more ingeniously, and they use fewer resources. For example, Google gives its engineers "20 percent time": they can work on whatever project they want for 20 percent of their time. More than half of the products and projects Google releases were created during this 20 percent time.

Other companies set up ROWEs (Results-Only Work Environments), in which employees don't have set schedules, all meetings are optional, and it's entirely up to employees how they spend their time working. They can choose to work from home, they can work from 2:00 AM to 6:00 AM if it suits them, and they can sculpt their job however they want, as long as the results benefit the company as a whole. Cali Ressler and Jody Thompson have defined and then studied ROWE implementations for over a decade, and they find that in these kinds of autonomous environments, productivity goes up, employee satisfaction goes up, and turnover goes down.

For entrepreneurs or those working for themselves, autonomy may seem easier to achieve but can come with several pitfalls. Often when you start working for yourself you trade micromanaging bosses for micromanaging clients. The solution to finding better clients and better projects has a lot to do with your skill and experience, just as I mentioned at the start of this section. When you're starting out and your skills aren't as developed, you won't be able to lead projects or be too picky about the type of work you do. But as your expertise increases and your network grows, you can land better clients — the kind who listen more carefully to how you would do what they're paying you to do — and you can be more selective about the types of customers and projects you want to take on.

Kaitlin Maud, a digital strategist and currently a freelancer, put in her time developing her skills at an agency for five years. She spent that time learning the ropes of her industry as well as building a solid network of contacts, with whom she actively kept in touch. Just like Tom the cartoonist, she didn't venture out on her own until she had enough freelance projects to bring in a relatively stable side income.

Kaitlin thinks that a sense of autonomy looks different on everyone. She herself has created a work life that rewards her for getting her work done quickly. In a typical company, regardless of how quickly you work, you're still required to be there for a set number of hours a day; in other words, there's no reward for productivity or efficiency. Kaitlin has also found that she's able to get work done with more focus from 9:00 AM to 1:00 PM, so she doesn't schedule meetings or calls during that window of time.

According to a study from Upwork, freelancing now accounts for more than one-third of jobs in America. Like Kaitlin, people are increasingly *choosing* to go freelance — that is, they're not using freelance work as a fallback because their job disappeared. Freelancing makes up almost half the jobs being done by younger people, who are choosing to freelance in hopes of gaining more control over their career path. As a society, we're gradually starting to view "work" not as a single place of employment, but as a series of engagements or projects. The millennial generation in particular views the traditional aspiration to a corporate job in an office as something like a satirical sitcom, à la *The Office,* than something they wish to strive for.

With a stable of side project clients and a vast network of contacts in hand, Kaitlin left her agency job and started to freelance full-time. When she started, she first worked at leveling up her skill set before focusing on becoming more autonomous. Since going solo, she's had a steady waiting list, regularly has to turn down projects that are a fit for her values, and has worked with some large companies like Beats by Dre, Taco Bell, Adobe, and Toms. Her work, because she put in the time to become great at it, now revolves around her life. She can focus entirely on the type of work she loves, solving problems with creative solutions online — basically, Kaitlin is the Olivia Pope (of *Scandal* fame) of the internet. She fixes things that no one else can — and she's well on her way to becoming her own company of one.

Sol Orwell, a fellow Canadian, has refused venture capital for his very profitable business, Examine.com, because he doesn't see an upside in relinquishing control to venture capitalists. He doesn't need cash — his company makes seven figures per year. He isn't looking for a quick out or trying to sell — he enjoys his work a great deal. As a majority owner, he doesn't have to answer to anyone except his paying customers. Sol would rather have ownership of his work and the freedom to not have to fill every minute of every day with his job. Success to him means making a great living, but not at the expense of being able to take long midday breaks to walk his dog or attend hourlong dance classes on a Wednesday afternoon.

But bear this in mind: achieving control over a company of one requires more than just using the core skill you are hired for. It also requires proficiency at sales, marketing, project management, and client retention. Whereas most normal corporate workers can be hyperfocused on a single skill, companies of one, even within a larger business, need to be generalists who are good at several things — often all at once.

Speed

Companies of one work best under constraints — because that's where creativity and ingenuity thrive. Companies like Basecamp have a four-day workweek during the summer (no work on Fridays) because it helps them prioritize what's important to work on and what they can let go of. The key for their employees is to figure out how to work smarter to accomplish tasks with the time they've got, not just harder. Companies of one question their systems, processes, and structure to become more efficient and to achieve more with the same number of employees and fewer hours of work.

On the company intranet, Basecamp has a "weekend check-in" where employees can post photos of what they did on their three days off from work. This helps this remote-based company build connections between its employees, who are spread all over the globe.

Speed is not merely about frantically working faster. It's about figuring out the best way to accomplish a task with new and efficient methods. This is the concept at work in the ROWE method: employees no longer have to work a set amount of time, but are rewarded when they finish their tasks faster. By being smarter at getting more work done faster when you work for yourself, you can create a more flexible schedule that fits work into your life in better ways.

Tasks that used to take Kaitlin days to accomplish in the open-office environment of the agency she worked at now take her only a few hours, because she's figured out what needs to be in place to maximize her productivity. This gives her the space in her workday, when she's not at peak productivity, to head to the gym or spend time with her newborn daughter. She's able to accomplish eight hours of agency work in four hours of freelance work, freeing up half her day. She still works hard and sometimes has to work much longer as project deadlines loom, but she enjoys the reality that most of the time on her schedule is her own.

Another aspect of speed in a company of one is the ability to pivot quickly when a customer base or market changes. As a solo worker or small company, a company of one finds this much easier to do, because it has less infrastructure to cut through.

So speed works to the advantage of companies of one not only because they're able to pivot when needed, and far faster, but also because they have less of the corporate mass that often gets in the way. Stewart Butterfield started out developing online games, like Game Neverending and Glitch. Both games failed to gain enough of an audience to become profitable, but both times Stewart was able to pivot his (then) small teams, pluck key features from the games, and spin them off into their own products — the photo-sharing site Flickr and Slack, an internal chat system that is now worth over $1 billion. Facing the limitations of both time and money running out, Stewart's teams managed to hyperfocus on a single solution and bring it to market. By keeping his company small and by paying attention to what was working and what wasn't, he was able to quickly move to spin-offs that ultimately netted great gains.

When I asked Danielle LaPorte if she'd take funding again for a new business idea, she said no. She'd learned that not accepting outside funding allowed her to move faster. Instead, she said, she would quickly release a first version of a new product that would fund iterations on it, keeping her costs and expenses as low as possible in order to move toward profitability as quickly as possible. The fewer staff and less external funding involved, the faster a company can move, whether forward or in a new, more promising direction.

Simplicity

The best example of the power of simplicity comes from two rival social bookmarking services, Pinboard and Delicious. Delicious grew quickly, adding lots of features, and its founder, Joshua Schachter, made investments early on and grew Delicious into a company with approximately 5.3 million users. The company was sold to Yahoo for somewhere between $15 million and $30 million. Unable to make it profitable, Yahoo sold it to Avos Systems, which removed the popular support forums that Delicious users had come to love. A few years later, Avos sold Delicious to Science, Inc., where Delicious users were continually leaving and using other services.

While Delicious was rapidly changing hands, Pinboard was started by web developer Maciej Ceglowski. He offered his simple service to users at $3 per year, a fee that increased over time to $11 per year. Since the beginning, Pinboard has been a one-person company with a limited feature-set and with no investors. Ceglowski operated it as a side business for the first few months, until it was generating enough income for him to move to working on Pinboard full-time.

Then, on June 1, 2017, Pinboard acquired Delicious for just $35,000 and quickly shut it down to new users, offering existing users the option to migrate their accounts to Pinboard instead.

After rapid growth and increased complexity in its offerings and internal structure, Delicious, in which millions of dollars had been invested, was ultimately consumed by a company of one for a tiny price. Pinboard had kept things simple, played the long game, and ended up winning.

Typically, as companies gain success or traction, they grow by taking on additional complexities. These complexities can often detract from a business's original or primary focus, resulting in more costs and the investment of more time and money.

For a company of one at any size, simple rules, simple processes, and simple solutions typically win. Complexity is often well intentioned, especially at large corporations, where, as complicated processes are added to other complicated processes and systems, accomplishing any task requires more and more work on the job and not toward finishing the task. It can be a slippery slope: one step is added to a process without increasing its complexity too much, but then, after a few years of adding steps here and there, a task that once took a handful of steps now requires sign-off by six department heads, a legal review, and a dozen or more meetings with stakeholders.

By contrast, growth for a company of one can mean simplifying rules and processes, which frees up time to take on either more work or more clients, because tasks can be finished faster. With this goal in mind, companies of one routinely question everything they do. *Is this process efficient enough? What steps can be removed and the end result will be the same or better? Is this rule helping or hindering our business?*

For a company of one to succeed, a strategy for simplifying isn't just a desirable goal but an absolute requirement. Having too many products or services, too many layers of management, and/ or too many rules and processes for completing tasks leads to atrophy. Simplicity has to be a mandate.

When Mike Zafirovski became the CEO of Nortel, he implemented an unambiguous theme of "business made simple" across the entire company. From reducing costs to speeding up product development, to making it easier for customers to get the latest technology, he wove the idea of "simple" into every aspect of their large company.

Often, complexity can creep in right from the beginning — when you're just thinking about starting a new business. You begin to assume that your business requires "essentials" like office space, websites, business cards, computers, fax machines (just kidding), and custom software solutions. In reality, it's usually possible to start a business — especially the freelance or startup kind — just by finding and then helping a single paying customer. Then doing it again, and again. And only adding new items or processes to the mix when they're absolutely required.

If you have an idea for starting a business that requires a lot of money, time, or resources, you're most likely thinking too big. Your idea can be scaled down to the basics — do it now, do it on the cheap, and do it quickly — and then iterated upon. Start without automation or infrastructure or overhead. Start by helping one customer. Then another. This puts your focus on helping people immediately with what you've got available to you right now. Work on things like sales funnels and automation when it no longer makes sense to personalize your interactions with your customers in surprising and delightful ways.

We've become enamored with new technologies, new software, and new devices, and too often large companies and even solo companies try to incorporate them into their existing structures in an effort to "keep up." The problem here is mistaking "simple" for "easy." Often we try to be simpler and end up more complicated. We add more tools, more software, more devices to the mix to make things easier, without testing or questioning how easy they'll be to use on a daily basis.

Even the latest and greatest HR software, for instance, probably doesn't need hundreds of screens and drop-down menus. A business selling thousands of products can probably cut most of them if the bulk of their sales comes from just 5 percent of their offerings. There may be no need for thirteen company-wide initiatives if three will do.

Start out as simple as possible, and always fervently question adding new layers of complexity. Set yourself up as a company of one that's run to maximize your ability to solve existing problems and to adapt as new problems arise. And then, who knows, perhaps you'll end up acquiring a massive competitor that couldn't keep up with your radical simplicity.

BEGIN TO THINK ABOUT:

- Whether growth is truly beneficial to your business
- How you could solve business problems without just adding "more"
- Whether you really need funding or venture capital for your idea, or are simply thinking too big to start

2

Staying Small as an End Goal

SEAN D'SOUZA DOESN'T WANT TO grow his company. He decided that $500,000 a year of profit was all he wanted to earn and that his business shouldn't exceed it. So that's what Psychotactics — his consultancy that teaches other businesses the psychology of why their customers buy (or don't buy) — earns through its website and in-person training workshops.

Sean feels that his job as a business owner is not to endlessly increase profits, or even to defeat the competition, but instead to create better and better products and services that his customers benefit from in their lives and work. Implementation, he's found, is the key to retaining his customers and persuading them to keep buying — that is, if they're using what he makes, they see successes in their own business and then keep buying more from him.

Sean is only interested in reaching his target limit. This goal feels very counterintuitive to what we're taught about business and success. Society says that business goals should focus on ever-increasing profit and that, as profit increases, so should everything else — more employees, more expenses, more growth. But like many others, Sean feels that the opposite is true — that success can be personally defined, and that while profit and sustainability are absolutely important to a business, they aren't the only driving forces, metrics, or factors in business success.

Sean's goal of achieving a target profit and not exceeding it comes from shaping his business around an optimal life he wants to lead — complete with taking a three-month vacation each year with his wife and spending hours walking, cooking, and teaching and tutoring his two young nieces each day.

Typically awake by 4:00 AM — no alarm clock required — Sean goes to work early from a small office located in his backyard. By starting this early, Sean can record audio for his podcast before the world around him becomes too noisy. It's an idyllic life filled with hourlong walks and ample coffee breaks. His work routine revolves mostly around answering questions for his customers in his private message board on his website.

Sean is easily able to meet his $500,000 per year profit goal, not through marketing and promotion, but by paying close attention to his existing customer base. His audience has grown slowly and sustainably because those listeners share his work with their own audiences and contacts — his current customers gladly become his (unpaid) sales force.

Too often businesses forget about their current audience — the people who are already listening, buying, and engaging. These should be the most important people to your business — far more so than anyone you wish you were reaching. Whether your audience is ten people, a hundred people, or even a thousand people, if you're not doing right by them, right now, nothing you do regarding growth or marketing will make a lick of difference. Make sure you're listening to, communicating with, and helping the people who are already paying attention to you.

Sean sees lots of people in the online education world focusing their time entirely on marketing, but his focus is on making his products better for his existing audience. He works to get more and better results for his existing customers, who in turn continue to buy from him, both established products and new products as he releases them. He likens his business to a kind of "Hotel California" — "You can check in anytime, but you can never leave" — except that his version is less psychedelically creepy and doesn't feature pink champagne on ice; it features chocolate.

Part of Sean's customer retention strategy involves sending his customers a box of chocolates, with a handwritten note and sometimes a small cartoon he draws himself. The package costs him approximately $20, which includes shipping from New Zealand (where he lives currently), but it's the one thing his customers talk about. They'll buy a $2,000 training program from him and talk about the chocolate. He'll give a speech at an event, and people will talk about the chocolate. His customers love these small touches, and the attention his business gives them, because his company of one focuses solely on serving his existing customers, not on infinite growth.

When a friend of Sean's had a remarkably profitable year, they cracked open the champagne (possibly pink champagne, on ice) in a meeting and vowed to double that profit in the following year. But Sean is absolutely certain that his end goal is to keep his business small. He questions the blind growth mind-set because he doesn't require it. If he were to double his profits, like his friend was trying to do, how much more work would be involved? How would that extra work affect his family or his life overall? Sean doesn't want that complexity, the added stress and responsibility. He'd much rather make a great living without his work taking over all aspects and hours of his life. So succeeding, for Sean, means staying small.

Sean's Psychotactics business is a great example of a company of one finding its optimum size and staying put. He purposely keeps his business small as a long-term strategy that makes sense for maximizing his profits and his lifestyle. With Psychotactics at its current size, he's able to get to know and better help his customers, who in turn are eager to spend thousands on his training products every year—as long as he also sends them $20 worth of chocolate.

Like Sean, Ricardo Semler, CEO of Semco Partners, has found the right organic size for the businesses he owns and invests in. And it's working for him, as he's grown Semco into a business worth more than $160 million. He believes that companies need to focus on becoming *better* instead of simply growing *bigger*. His approach is to question the idea that growth is always good and always unlimited. Ricardo works at determining the size at which each company he manages can enjoy worldwide competitive advantages and then stop growth from there in order to turn the focus away from getting bigger and toward getting better instead.

The current business paradigm teaches us that to make a lot of money or to achieve lasting success, we need to scale our businesses—as if larger businesses are less prone to fail or to become unprofitable (obviously not true). In fact, according to this view, before our imagined businesses are even off the ground we need to create them with the sole purpose of growth—and possibly eventual sale for a huge profit. This paradigm, however, isn't rooted in truth, nor does it hold up to critical investigation.

A study done by the Startup Genome Project, which analyzed more than 3,200 high-growth tech startups, found that 74 percent of those businesses failed, not because of competition or bad business plans, but because they scaled up too quickly. Growth, as a primary focus, is not only a bad business strategy, but an entirely harmful one. In failing—as defined in the study—these high-growth startups had massive layoffs, closed shop completely, or sold off their business for pennies on the dollar. Putting growth over profit as a strategy, however trendy as business advice, was their downfall.

When the Kauffman Foundation and Inc. magazine did a follow-up study on a list of the 5,000 fastest-growing companies five to eight years later, they found that more than two-thirds of them were out of business, had undergone massive layoffs, or had been sold below their market value, confirming the findings of the Startup Genome Project. These companies weren't able to become self-sustaining because they spent and grew based on where they thought their revenue would hit — or they grew based on venture capital injections of funds, not on where revenues were actually at.

Venture capital can be a quick way to infuse money into a company to help it succeed, but it's not a requirement and it definitely comes with certain pitfalls. The Kauffman Foundation study also illustrated that almost 86 percent of companies that succeeded in the long term did *not* take VC money. Why? Because a company's interests may not always align with the interests of its backers. Worse, investor interests may not always align with what's best for a business's end customers. Capital infusion can also leave a business with less control, resilience, speed, and simplicity — the main traits required for companies of one.

Paul Graham, the cofounder of Y Combinator (one of the largest and most notable VC firms for startups) explains that VCs don't invest millions in companies because that's what those companies might need; rather, they invest the amount that their own VC business requires to see growth in their own portfolios, coming from the few companies that actually give them a positive return. Graham notes that sudden and large investments tend to turn companies into "armies of employees who sit around having meetings."

Startups, as serial entrepreneur Salim Ismail states, are extremely fragile by nature. They're designed to be temporary organizations that *may* grow into large companies, under conditions of extreme uncertainty. They expend money and resources in the anticipation that revenue will catch up to spending. Most startups fail because that doesn't happen often.

Although a lot of these examples involve companies that would be considered startups, companies of one aren't always startups in the traditional sense. Many startups focus on growth, buyouts, employees, lavish offices with foosball tables and open-concept floor plans, and massive profits at any cost, and they tend to rely on investors for initial cash. Companies of one instead focus on stability, simplicity, independence, and long-term resilience and rely on starting small and becoming as profitable as possible, without the need for outside investment. Companies of one, with their focus on what can be done in the here and now, not what can be done with investment, can also be started without an injection of capital.

Not all startups can be lumped together — some are challenging the mantras of blind startup growth. For instance, Buffer, a social media scheduling tool with more than three million users, has seventy-two employees and isn't looking to grow that number quickly, unless it absolutely has to. Buffer wasn't always in the mind-set of challenging growth — a few years ago the company got caught up in a hiring frenzy because it was looking to do a large round of raising capital. The idea was to be ambitious in hiring in order to do more to capture more of the market share and hit new revenue targets that investors were going to want to see. But Buffer hired more people than it had revenue to pay.

Two shifts then happened: Buffer realized that even after securing funding, it still had to lay off 11 percent of the team. That employees could be hired and paid based on revenue targets (instead of on actual and current profits) wasn't a reasonable assumption to have made. Second, they realized that their leadership team was divided about what success meant to their company. The CEO wanted a more profit-driven, holistic, slow-growth plan and believed in hiring more employees only when the money was there, not in the hopes that it would materialize. Buffer's COO and CTO, by contrast, were more motivated by high stakes and high growth — in other words, the typical startup game. In the end, they left the company and no other employees left or were let go; those who remained shared their CEO's vision of slower, profit-based growth.

When businesses require endless growth to turn a profit, it can be difficult to keep up with increasingly higher targets. Whereas, if a business turns a good profit at its current size, then growth can be a choice, made when it makes sense to succeed, and not a requirement for success.

For companies of one, the question is always *what can I do to make my business better?*, instead of *what can I do to grow my business larger?*

THE DOWNSIDE OF EXCESSIVE GROWTH AS AN END GOAL

Often, in the pursuit of growth, companies or founders have to battle what Danielle LaPorte refers to as "the Beast." A company focused on growth often puts into place complicated systems to handle exponential volume and scale, which require more re-sources (human and financial) to manage, which then require more complex systems to manage the increased resources, and so on and so on.

Danielle's "Beast" was the system and structure (financial and technological) she created to match her grand vision for her busi-ness. She invested in a million-dollar website to take her business to the next level. The problem was that a million-dollar website requires a team of experts to manage and run it at all times. Up-dating blog posts or products can incur tremendous costs.

The Beast had an ever-growing appetite and required constant feeding. To keep the Beast satiated, Danielle's focus was pulled away from her center — that is, from her purpose in creating and running a business in the first place. As her focus became muddied she found herself busier with feeding the Beast than in taking care of her core business. When Danielle realized that she didn't want to exponentially grow to continue feeding the Beast, she decided it had to be destroyed.

In "killing her own Kraken," as she put it, she began to radically simplify. Her strategy shifted from "broadcasting light . . . to as many people as possible" to "broadcasting light . . . to the people with eyes to see it." Not focusing on growth and scale, she believes, was the best way to remove the Beast from her company of one and return her focus to the people who were already paying attention to her work. She likens her decision to stop trying to reach infinitely more people through paid channels to feeding only those people who show up for dinner — the ones who naturally or organically find her work through word of mouth or who are hanging out where her business hangs out. The fact is that she still has hundreds of thousands of ravenous fans showing up for "dinner."

Lusting after the Beast, of course, feels completely understandable and human — even in business, we all need to feel loved and wanted, some of us more than others. However, unless we truly question this need and how relevant it is to our business, we can perish because of it. Buddhists call the Beast the "hungry ghost" — a pitiable creature with an insatiable appetite. There is never enough for the hungry ghost, so it's always looking for more. In business, the hungry ghost is the quest for more growth, more profit, more followers, more likes.

Even large and established companies aren't immune to the perils of chasing the Beast of high and infinite growth. Starbucks, Krispy Kreme, and Pets.com all pursued aggressive scaling and have paid a steep price in various ways.

Starbucks was opening hundreds of stores around the world but decided that it could scale faster by adding sandwiches, CDs, and fancier drinks to its offerings. This rapid expansion ended up diluting the Starbucks brand, and in an equally rapid contraction, the company was forced to close 900 stores. Subsequently, Starbucks returned its focus to doing its one thing — coffee — better. It renewed its efforts to recapture a boutique coffee shop experience by upgrading coffee machinery, retraining staff in the art of making a perfect espresso shot, and removing a lot of the superfluous products like music and lunch food. Starbucks learned the hard way that better isn't always bigger.

Krispy Kreme's freshly cooked novelty treats were so popular (and delicious) that it seemed like the company couldn't fail. Its freshly baked sign would regularly lead to lines that went on for blocks. But in focusing on expansion into grocery stores, gas stations, and even multiple locations in small areas, Krispy Kreme diluted the very scarcity it had once capitalized on. As franchises were pitted against each other, the company found itself chasing diminishing profits: it dropped 18 percent in sales over the two years from 2004 to 2006. Krispy Kreme's newly massive size also created some accounting and reporting nightmares that forced it into a $75 million settlement with the U.S. Securities and Exchange Commission.

Finally, Pets.com is, by most measures, the epitome of the dot-com boom-and-bust cycle — an example of prioritizing uncontrolled and overfunded growth while doing things like selling products far below cost (which obviously isn't sustainable). Pets.com spent more than $17 million on advertising involving sock puppets in the second quarter of 2000 alone; meanwhile, their revenue (not profit) at that time was only $8.8 million. Pets.com was spending based on growth it *hoped* to see, not on where the company was *currently* at, and it ended up losing an estimated $300 million in investment capital along the way.

Of course, economies of scale can sometimes be required for success in certain markets and for some products, but often they aren't required and it is ego, not a strong business strategy, that is forcing growth where growth isn't necessary.

When you feel like you have to start out competing with the largest player in the market, you end up chasing your competitor's growth instead of bettering your own offering. Sometimes finding and working with a single customer, then adding another, and then another, is a very useful and solid way to begin. And sometimes that can even be the end goal — one where your focus is on the relationship and the paid work at hand. Sometimes the best plan is focused on your current customers' success, not on chasing leads and growth.

Not everything needs to scale to succeed — as Leah Andrews, founder of Queen of Snow Globes, discovered almost by accident. She runs an extremely unscalable business: creating intricate and unique snow globes, one at a time, for her customers. From the start, she was inundated with requests for these custom pieces of art, from big names like Quentin Tarantino and Channing Tatum and even from Netflix's corporate offices. Instead of scaling production, she focused on raising her prices higher and higher until the demand leveled off to where she could handle orders. She focused on creating an amazing product that was better than the competition — mass-produced snow globes — and was able to charge a huge premium for her work. Because she focused on making the best product, not the most scalable product, she grew her profits quickly without scaling production, which would have also scaled complexity and expenses.

Pat Riley, the Hall of Fame basketball coach who led five teams to the NBA championship, coined the term "the disease of more." He noticed time and time again that winning players, just like some startups, focused on *more* instead of *better.* Once they won, they'd let their own ego get in the way of all the tasks that had helped them win in the first place — like practice and focus — and instead become lured into more endorsements, more accolades, and more media attention. As a result, they ultimately lost to internal forces, not to competitors.

When you focus on doing business and serving customers in better and better ways, your company of one can end up profiting more from the same amount of work because you can raise the prices until your demand flattens out to where you can handle it. I did the same when my business was a client-focused design business: I doubled my rates over and over until the demand only slightly exceeded the time I had available to do the work. In doing so, I didn't need to hire more people to grow profits; I just needed to focus on doing better and better work—putting in the same number of hours but vastly increasing the revenue generated from the work I did. Staying small is still my end goal, because like Sean's and Ricardo's visions for corporate success, I look toward betterment instead of infinite scalability.

There's nothing wrong with finding the right size and then focusing on being better. Small can be a long-term plan, not just a stepping-stone.

IS THE TRADITIONAL WAY OF DOING BUSINESS BROKEN?

Traditional ways of working—in offices with strict rules and corporate hierarchies—are giving way to gig-based, remote work with more autonomy. The business world is constantly being disrupted with new automations and technologies, and this is a good thing. Changes in how we work give us a chance to scale with the bare minimum in investments, people, and time.

Traditionally, having a small business was thought of as a good starting point, or as what happens when a business finds only limited success. But there's a new breed of business that starts small and stays small, and not for lack of vision or strategy, but because these days one person (or a tiny team) can accomplish a lot. Technology is constantly improving, allowing us to do things like automate sales funnels, or drop-ship physical products with no need for warehouses and staff, or print-on-demand without investing in machinery and storage.

WordPress, the software that powers 26 percent of all websites on the internet, closed its gorgeous San Francisco office, not because the company was out of money (it's extremely profitable) but because employees were barely working at the office, opting instead to work at home. The 15,000-square-foot WordPress office was being used by approximately five people a day; having 3,000 square feet to work in is definitely a bit too much space. Because technology makes it easy to work from anywhere, on any computer, less spending on overhead (like offices and the things that come with offices) is required.

Pieter Levels is a digital nomad and Dutch programmer who is challenging the status quo of business tradition. Working from any location around the globe with an internet connection (currently in a village in Thailand), he builds software that competes with VC-funded Silicon Valley companies with teams of twenty or more people. Pieter runs his online service, Nomad List — a community list of cities around the world ranked by how easy and fun it is to work from them — and earns $400,000 a year without employees or even an office. With the *New York Times, Wired,* CNN, and *Forbes* having all reported on Nomad List, Pieter needs no PR or marketing team, just a focus on a great and always improving service. Because the company is just Pieter and a handful of contractors he uses as he needs them, he can implement ideas as he has them, test them to see if there's a market fit, and quickly pivot if there's not. He's able to be top of his industry, above much larger companies, as a team of one — and he currently doesn't even have a traditional mailing address. By automating what he can with existing software, he's even able to be offline for weeks at a time and still have steady revenues.

Through careful planning and strategically executing personalized sales funnels, people like Brennan Dunn, who runs an email automation and training consultancy, are able to launch products without even lifting a finger. Brennan can leave home, not even bringing a computer, and still have record sales because he's built a system that drives ideal buyers to his website, converts them into subscribers, sends them personalized emails that change content based on their actions or behavior on the site and list, and finally turns them into buyers. It's a process that generates revenue whether or not he's present, and it's all done through software (email service providers like MailChimp or Drip) that costs a few hundred dollars a month to use. Brennan started down the traditional path of hiring employees, having an office, and scaling people, investments, and resources to get his business to succeed. But now that he's scaled back to having no office and only a handful of remote contractors, he spends less time on work — and far less on overhead — and generates more revenue by using off-the-digital-shelf technology.

Tools that used to be expensive enterprise software — or hadn't even been developed yet — today are cheap, easy to master, and easy to use without spending a lot of time on them. For example, I can run a 30,000-person mailing list that generates the bulk of my income by spending approximately an hour a week on it. I can create a document that's both editable and shareable around the world for free with Google Documents or share any file, of any size, using a service like Dropbox. I can replace an entire IT department with one on-contract systems administrator in Berlin who works one to two hours a month for me, and I can learn everything I need to know about the visitors to the websites that run my business with free analytics software. Technology has made it easy to do what used to cost thousands or require a team of people. The new reality of business makes it easier than ever to be a company of one and not have massive growth as an end goal.

Working for Yourself: Too Risky?

Risk isn't just the name of a famous, amazing, and all-consuming board game — it's what most people think is involved in working for yourself! And sure, there is definitely risk that can't be mitigated in working for yourself, but we should challenge the idea that being your own company of one is riskier than working at a traditional company.

Just as the traditional way of doing business is changing, the outdated, fear-ridden assumption that entrepreneurialism is a hazardous venture needs to change as well. In today's world, there is no longer the single track to security of going to school, getting a degree, and finding and keeping a job until retirement. Jobs and career tracks are no longer as secure as they were decades ago. Quite simply, the days of throwing retirement parties for employees of fifty years and sending them off with a gold watch and a great pension are long gone.

Miranda Hixon, founder and principal of MilkWood Designs, does workspace design for small startups in the Bay Area. Think of her work as intentional workspace design based on a company's specific internal style and communication style — basically the physical manifestation of a company's culture. Her role with clients can include buying or custom-making beautiful furniture pieces, planning the organization of a space, and adjusting a space as a company experiences growth spurts or downsizing.

Growing up in the 1980s, Miranda dreamed of wearing power suits to a corporate job. (Hey, both were the rage back then.) When she was a child, her father, Steve Hixon, began working for himself after being laid off from a large architecture firm. The job he was forced to leave was supposed to be stable and secure, but when businesses or economies change, large companies downsize — something most employees have no control over.

Miranda's father ran his new project management business

from the family garage in the suburbs of San Francisco — a win-
dowless room the family referred to as "the Box," as in, "Where's
Dad? Is he out in the Box?" In this not-so-luxurious home office
was the one and only family computer, and stuck to the monitor
was a Post-it that read "OVERHEAD = DEATH," which was his
philosophy for running the business. Far ahead of his time, he
kept things small by using a network of freelance architects, engineers, and estimators, and only as he needed them. Since the
company was just him, he was also able to pivot several times
when shifts in the market and specific types of work he enjoyed
doing led him to niches to focus on. Keeping his company of one
small (just him) enabled him to set his own flexible hours, so he
could coach Miranda's swim and basketball teams on some days
and then work in the evenings instead.

Miranda made her first foray into a postschool career with
startups in Silicon Valley. While she enjoyed the friendships,
travel, and community these jobs gave her, she also found herself hitting a glass ceiling fairly hard. Although the mostly white,
wealthy, and male leadership preached total inclusivity and open
values to their communities, she was constantly met with resistance on her own career growth. This led her to venture out on
her own, where she could be more autonomous and have more
control over the limits to her career — or scrap them altogether.

Her father's "OVERHEAD = DEATH" mentality seeped into
Miranda's subconsciousness, and she runs her business as he ran
his. She hires painters, movers, installation workers, and carpen-
ters only as she needs them, and from a pool of trusted people
with whom she's worked in the past or who have been referred
to her directly. She also pays them above-average wages to incentivize them to work on smaller projects or on weekends. Because
she pays them what she feels is fair, they do better-than-aver-
age work, for which she can charge her clients a premium. And

by keeping her business small, she's able to work in a niche — smaller startups — that interior design firms with lots of employees and overhead have to avoid as they chase higher revenues.

Her childhood vision of power suits in corner offices died off, not because shoulder pads are no longer in vogue, but because she realized that constant growth often brings on stress and anxiety. When you hire employees, you're responsible for them. You're their source of income that goes toward paying their mortgages, feeding their families, and even sending their children to college. That's a heavy responsibility. But keeping people on contract as freelancers makes you responsible for them only for a specific project, and you know that what you're getting paid includes what you'll pay them.

Miranda has found a way to have enough responsibility to succeed on her own terms, but not so much responsibility that she becomes stressed and has to spend lots of time managing others. Able to retreat for long stretches of time to a yurt she built in the Sierra Nevada foothills, she finds that her overall life is less stressed as well.

I've worked for myself for nearly twenty years and have had stable, increasing income every single year. That's in direct contrast to many of my friends who have worked at larger companies or startups and been laid off or downsized every time the economy changes. In the United States, the number of non-employee establishments (people who work for themselves and have no employees) with an annual revenue of $1 million grew by nearly 6 percent in 2015, according to the U.S. Census Bureau. It found that 38,029 companies (of one) were bringing in seven-figure revenues, doing everything from the usual high-tech and scientific work to equipment repair and laundry services.

The Census Bureau data shows that each year it becomes easier and less risky to work for yourself and still make a decent living. You can outsource or hire freelancers to cover tasks that were traditionally done by an employee. And unlike a corporation, you, as the boss, can't be downsized or hit a gender-based glass ceiling. As long as you're doing great work that's in demand, working for yourself has no limits — or, as we'll see next, only smart upper limits that you put in place yourself.

UPPER BOUNDS

Most businesses set goals and targets, but few consider having an upper bound to them. Paying attention instead to the lower bound of a goal, they focus on ever-exceeding increases in areas like profit and reach and set goals like, "I want to make at least $1 million this quarter," or, "We need to grow our mailing list by 2,000 people per day." They set the minimum threshold they want to reach, with the implication that if more happens, that's even better.

What if we set upper limits to our goals instead? For instance, "I want to make at least $1 million this quarter, but *not more than $1.4 million*," or, "We need to grow our list by 2,000 people per day, *but not more than 2,200*"?

In most areas of business, there's a magic zone for sustainability that relates to the concept brought up at the start of this book about having "enough." If growth happens too quickly, problems can arise — like not being able to hire fast enough to keep up, or not having enough infrastructure to handle increased volume. The lower limit can be important, for example, if you need to make enough revenue to be profitable. But more than that? How useful is it to make more than you need to be profitable? How does it benefit you, your business, or your customers if you blow past your company's goals?

James Clear, a successful blogger on the topic of habits and productivity, tells the story of Southwest Airlines being faced with an interesting problem way back in 1996: the airline had methodically expanded from a tiny regional carrier to having a bit more of a national presence. And at a time when most other airlines were losing money or going under, over 100 cities were begging Southwest to service their location. However, that's not the interesting part. What's interesting is that Southwest turned down over 95 percent of those offers and began serving only four new locations. It turned down exponential growth because company leadership had set an upper limit for growth.

Sure, Southwest's executives wanted to grow each year, but they didn't want to grow too much. Unlike Starbucks, Krispy Kreme, and Pets.com, they wanted to set their own pace, one that could be sustained in the long term. By doing this, they established a safety margin for growth that helped them continue to thrive at a time when the other airlines were flailing.

Southwest is interesting because its leaders did what they could to sustain their business, and not more. From an evolutionary point of view, there's probably a good reason to want to accumulate more and more. With more food, more water, more protection against predators, and so on, we may be less likely to die (probably by being eaten by something larger than us). So in the past, not having an upper bound to our goals served us well and kept us fed, protected, and evolving. But now, in modern society, having goals that grow and grow without limit can often be problematic. Most of us don't have to worry about food or protection, but we're still wired to want to collect more and more without end. This mind-set carries over to the businesses we create and run as well.

Culturally, growth feeds our ego and social standing. The bigger the company you own, with more profits and more employees than the next person, the better you might feel. James Clear figured that 10,000 subscribers to his new blog's newsletter would be the magic number that would signify his success. But then he hit 10,000 quickly and nothing in his blogging business changed.

He adjusted his goal to 100,000 subscribers, but still, when he quickly hit that number, nothing changed. As much as we don't want to be, or admit to being, guided by external factors and peer pressure in setting goals, to some degree we are. It's good to feel accepted and valued by a group. If our goals were completely internalized at all times, we wouldn't chase growth as much as we do. Even James now focuses on upper and lower bounds for his business and lets his goals be guided partially by the reasons for his work (as well as a little bit by external and peer factors).

ENVY: THE ULCER OF THE SOUL (AND OF BUSINESS GROWTH)

Socrates said that envy is the ulcer of the soul, meaning that we can easily become negatively affected by the success of others. Who we are and what we actually want become overshadowed when we internally compare ourselves to others. We idolize people like Steve Jobs, Elon Musk, and Oprah and think that their path to success — creating massive empires — is our own key to happiness and career fulfillment.

For some reason, when our business is just us, or when it isn't growing, we feel a societal pressure to keep up with other, larger businesses in order to be seen as "making it." After a person answers the question "What do you do?" by saying that they work for themselves, the second question is typically "How big is your business?" You may be slightly embarrassed if you have to answer that the business is just you and that you have no plans to grow. Really, though, running a business of any size is hard work. Having made it sustainable and profitable, whether it's big or small, should be something to be proud of.

External pressure and even some internal wishing for growth mostly comes from this envy. We see another business and assume that, if it's large, that business has made it. Even very transparent companies typically share only their gross numbers or MRR (monthly recurring revenue), which is only a small part of the picture and doesn't account for what their actual profit or margins are. A business that's making $500,000 a month could be hemorrhaging key staff due to overworking, and its burn rate could be $550,000 a month — making it unprofitable and potentially unsustainable once the VC money runs out.

Envy is hard to manage, as it's a socially unacceptable emotion, even though it's something most people feel. Envy also takes the focus off your work, your business, and your customers. When we give in to envious feelings, the best we can hope for is second best, since we're focused on copying someone else's path and not forging our own.

Envy is also based on a false comparison, like comparing uncooked ingredients to a delicious baked pie. Envying others, we see only the end result or the final product — the delicious dessert. But in ourselves, we see all the not-so-tasty starting ingredients and are aware of all the real work required to combine them into a successful end product. We too often compare our sometimes messy selves to only the best and shiniest part of others and come up short. Remember, every business has not only its successes but also its failures.

But there is one way that envy can be useful: as a tool to recognize in ourselves what we truly value. For example, if I'm envious that you make more money than I do, then I need to recognize that making more money might be important to me, work toward figuring out if that's truly the case, and then, if it is, determine how I can best make more of it. Once we learn what triggers our envy, we can focus on how to rethink or move forward.

In an ancient language from India called Pali, there's a term, "mudita," which seems like the opposite of envy, because it means "to delight in the good fortunes or the accomplishments of others." (Interestingly, it has no counterpart in English.) Outside of altruism, mudita is useful in business: we can be pleased that people like Musk or Oprah exist and thrive, while at the same time not letting their prolifically growing empires affect what we do or how we see our own businesses. We can be open to the insight that others have their own business successes but are not the sole factor in steering our own.

We don't need an attitude of world domination and crushing it in our work in order to make a great living or even have a substantial impact. Our work can start and finish small while still being useful — focused on moving toward better instead of more.

BEGIN TO THINK ABOUT:

- Whether you are paying attention to your existing customers or to just your potential customers
- Whether you could make your business better (however you define that) instead of just making it bigger
- Whether your business really needs scale to succeed
- Where the upper bound to that scale might be, the place where profit and enjoyment have diminishing returns
- How you could turn envy of others into enjoying their successes and learning from them

3

■

What's Required to Lead

SO FAR, WE'VE TOUCHED ON what a company of one is and why betterment of your quality of life should be valued above blind growth. Now we can turn our attention to who should lead a company of one and what specific traits are required—whether as an entrepreneur going solo, with no desire to hire others, or as the leader of an agile and autonomous team within a larger company.

What's required to lead a company of one may be different from what you think is called for, and we'll also look at the worrisome burdens of leadership and power—and how to avoid them.

THE NOT-SO-TYPICAL LEADER

Business and Hollywood share a prototypical vision of what a leader should be—a charismatic, dominant, type-A person (in most cases, a male) who commands attention simply by being the loudest and most vocal person in a room. That kind of leader can sometimes have a place, but it's not the only possible kind of leader (especially the being-male part). Companies of one can be led and run by quiet, thoughtful, introspective folks, even when there's a team to manage.

Companies of one do require leadership. If you work for yourself, you've got to be a leader to successfully pitch your services or products, as well as maintain relationships with clients or customers. If you work with a team of contractors or freelancers, then you've got to be able to lead them as well. Within a corporate setting, you cannot gain the control, resilience, and speed required to be autonomous without demonstrating leadership, even when corporate structure says that leadership is not your role.

Charisma — the so-called X-factor that leaders are supposed to be born with in order to make compelling pitches, inspire urgency, and encourage cooperation — isn't an innate quality that you either have or don't have. In fact, charisma can be taught or brought out when required, even in quiet individuals. Research from the University of Lausanne business school showed that training managers in a specific set of traits improved their charismatic qualities (even if they had no such inherent qualities) and thus their overall effectiveness as leaders. By using stories and metaphors, high expectations, and even facial expressions, anyone can employ and gain charisma to inspire others.

Another quality that helps is setting extremely high goals — for yourself and for others. Gandhi, in his famous "Quit India" speech, inspired an entire nation to liberate themselves from British rule without using violence. Katsuhiko Machida, the former CEO of Sharp, energized his employees in 1999, when their business faced collapse, by telling them the unthinkable: that all CRT televisions (those massive, clunky, deep boxes that TVs used to be) would have to be replaced by much thinner LCD models by 2005 to meet consumer demands. But setting these almost outrageous goals and expectations was not enough; they had to be accompanied by the confidence that they could be achieved. Gandhi did this through countless examples of peaceful protest, and Machida did it by convincing his engineering team that they could achieve this goal and that he trusted them to do so, and by giving them the resources to realize it.

Because Mark Zuckerberg, the CEO of Facebook, is a classic introverted leader, he enlists the help of COO Sheryl Sandberg, who offers him social and political guidance. Mark leans on smaller, genuine, collaborative connections rather than attempting to keep a large number of employees or subordinates under his rule. He's also been very competent at persuading other start-ups and their founders (typically very entrepreneurial in spirit) to join Facebook, by spending a lot of time with them and listening keenly.

A study done by professors at Harvard Business School found that introverted leaders, especially when they are managing skilled and proactive teams, can be highly successful. That's because a quieter, calmer leader is more likely to listen carefully, stay very focused, and not be afraid to work for long stretches of time without interruption. And they are able to lead a team of people who can do the same. Just as autonomy can only be of benefit once a skill set is mastered (as we discussed in Chapter 1), a company of one that operates as a small team requires real expertise from each member if they are to function both separately and as a whole without very much managing required.

This research from Adam Grant, Francesca Gino, and David Hofmann suggests that introverts can make better bosses — and that extroverted leaders, who sometimes speak first and think later, can actually lose the respect of their team, leading to poorer results. However, any leaders who listen carefully and are receptive to smart and useful suggestions from their team, whether they're introverted or extroverted, can build the trust required to earn cooperation.

Introverted leaders do have to overcome the strong cultural presumption that extroverts are more effective leaders. Although the population splits into almost equal parts between introverts and extroverts, more than 96 percent of managers and executives are extroverted. In a study done in 2006, 65 percent of senior corporate executives viewed introversion as a barrier to leadership. We must reexamine this stereotype, however, as it doesn't always hold true. Regent University found that a desire to be of service to others and to empower them to grow is a key factor in becoming a leader and retaining leadership. So-called servant leadership, dating back to ancient philosophy and the *Tao Te Ching*, adheres to the belief that a company's goals are best achieved by helping workers or customers achieve their goals. Such leaders do not seek attention but rather want to shine a light on others' wins and achievements. Servant leadership requires humility, but that humility ultimately pays off. Companies of one recognize that elevating others elevates the entire team or business.

Companies of one are sometimes quiet people who are internally motivated to make a difference in the world without shouting. Many people think they aren't the type of person who could start and run a business or inspire others to work with them or buy from them. I myself am the first to admit that I'm socially awkward and not well spoken in groups—I have a hard time functioning at everything from conferences to parties. What I have done is structure my business around what I'm better at —online teaching and written communication. I've turned my introversion into a positive tool, instead of an excuse for inaction. I find ways to lead that suit my personality and skill set: I avoid speaking to large groups and instead lean more on one-to-one communication. My introverted nature is the primary reason I teach online courses instead of doing speaking gigs. Online courses allow me to use a channel through which I can communicate effectively, and in a way that my audience connects with.

Since my practically nonexistent ability to lead could easily be a detriment to my company of one, I only work with freelancers and contractors who don't require management of any kind. They're A-players who know exactly how to get their work done. I simply need to provide them with the parameters and let them do their work. I give the people I hire full autonomy to do their jobs so I can do mine, with no need for meetings, or check-ins, or management. I ask them to let me know if a problem comes up; if I don't hear from them, I assume that their silence means they're accomplishing their tasks. I let my perceived shortcomings, like being awkward or bad at managing others, work for my business, not against it. My leadership style may require that I spend more when I hire (A-players come at a premium), but their work is always worth it and nets a positive return for my business.

AUTONOMY ISN'T A MAGIC BULLET

Leading a company of one that allows its workers to have autonomy isn't as simple as removing all rules, processes, and prescriptions. The result of that would be anarchy, which would be terrible for profitability and sustainability.

Today 79 percent of companies in the *Fortune* 1,000 and 81 percent of manufacturing organizations have empowered, self-directed, or autonomous teams, all of which are still led or managed in some way. It might seem odd that self-directed teams require direction, but in reality, they do require a specific type of direction.

Henrik Kniberg, a management coach who's worked with LEGO and Spotify, believes that assuming an organization can have either full autonomy or full alignment (where tasks for employees strictly align to the goals and directives of their managers) amounts to a false dichotomy. A bit of each is required, both for starting a business and maintaining it. A leader of a company of one has the role of enabling autonomy while providing alignment-setting processes and making sure there are common goals. Achieving this delicate balance can be challenging.

Kyle Murphy, the vice president of design at Hudl (a sports team software company), has gone from being the company's very first hire to one of 600 employees over the last nine years. When Hudl started, there was "autonomy overload" — every team worked on whatever they wanted, sometimes duplicating work and sometimes creating deliverables that didn't even fit together with other teams. This created chaos. What Kyle quickly identified was a need for global organization systems — not so much to limit the creativity and ingenuity of employees as to give them a common framework and playbook to work from.

Kyle's design team was struggling to hire enough designers to cover the amount of design work their company had to do and their current needs. This led Kyle to rethink the way in which Hudl's design team was operating, which was mostly as a flat group. By establishing rules like a common style guide for visual elements in their software (buttons, colors, fonts, etc.), Hudl needed fewer designers to do more work, because they now had a common set of building blocks. He also streamlined how feedback and revisions worked, so less time was required for those processes. In effect, hiring more people ended up not being the solution; instead, introducing more processes and structure helped fewer people accomplish more — while allowing them the autonomy to solve problems in their own way, using a common tool set.

Autonomy can also be badly abused. The problem is not so much employees taking advantage of perks like flex hours or remote work, but leaders assuming that they need to give less direction. A leader's job is to provide clear direction and then get out of the way. Even companies of one require direction and set processes — it's this common constraint that allows creativity to thrive and goals to be met. This alignment has to be carefully orchestrated, not as binary autonomous/non-autonomous decisions, but as a balance between guidance and trust. Provide too much guidance and a team will start to rely on it and leadership will become a bottleneck for decision-making. Provide too little and things devolve into anarchy. The middle ground is where high-performing teams excel, providing the most benefit to a company and delivering the most innovative and amazing results.

Even a company without employees still requires constraints. In serving clients with very specific deliverable requirements as well as customers who need your product to perform in a precise way, the more you can lean on processes, systems, and reusable building blocks (from code to marketing language to visuals) in your leadership, the better and faster you'll be with your work and the less you'll require in terms of hours worked or people hired, even as you gain more in terms of revenue, finished processes, and paid customers.

A VARIED SET OF SKILLS

In school and work, we're often taught that specialization is better and a key to success. From a young age, we're asked to pick a track that will lead us to a specific profession. In our jobs, we often use only one specific skill set to accomplish the tasks we're assigned. This is helpful in gaining domain expertise in a subject, but companies of one truly need to be able to know and understand a multitude of topics and skills in order to be in control of their work.

As a good generalist, you'll usually start with a specialization and then add auxiliary and complementary skills as needed, until you're able to understand all or most aspects of the business as a whole, not just one specific job within it. This is especially true when you work for yourself: you've got to know the skill you use to get paid or build the products you sell, but you also need to have a thorough understanding of key facets like marketing, bookkeeping, and sales.

In business, conditions are, of course, never perfect. In fact, they're typically less than ideal, with changing markets, differing trends, and consumer demand often flip-flopping. Specialists in the corporate world can thrive during certain surges. For instance, COBOL programmers were in demand in 1999 as Y2K approached — but then that need quickly diminished on January 1, 2000. In contrast, generalist programmers, who can write code in any language, have been in demand since computers started to become mainstream in the 1980s, and they have continued to see demand for their varied skill set.

According to Carter Phipps, author of *Evolutionaries*, generalists will continue to thrive in business as it becomes increasingly valuable to know "a little bit about a lot." Where you fall on the spectrum of generalist to specialist could therefore be the most important aspect of your survival as a company of one. Vikram Mansharamani, a lecturer at Yale, said that acknowledging specific expertise is overvalued. There are certainly domains, like hard science, that require specific knowledge, but for the most part specialist knowledge, if it is blind to everything else, just can't work in the business world today (or in companies of one) because there is too much uncertainty and ambiguity and metrics are so poorly defined. The time is at hand to embrace generalist thinking and the understanding of many things.

A generalist company of one leader needs to understand quite a few aspects of work to succeed. Not only do such leaders need to be masters at their core skill set, but they also need to understand how business works in general. There are a few leadership qualities of generalization that the leader of a company of one should either have to begin with or be willing to cultivate.

Psychology

Being able to understand how others think is critically important to a company of one. You need to know how and why people make decisions about your products or services. What leads them to buy what you create? What makes them hesitate? Where do they place value in their lives? If they do buy from you, what is considered a win for them? Where does churn happen in your business and why? Understanding these key factors can make you a better leader, a better salesperson, and a better marketer.

Communication

Even though we may not think we're communicators or writers, most of us spend a large portion of our days writing. Everything from emails to tweets to talking on the phone is communication. The more we can learn about how to communicate clearly and effectively, the better we'll be at leading, as our directives will be better understood.

Resilience

Miles Kington, a British journalist, reportedly said that "knowledge is knowing that a tomato is a fruit. Wisdom is not putting it in a fruit salad." We should never assume that having an abundance of knowledge is the same as having an abundance of wisdom. Even if you have access to a plethora of data or experience, there are still so many factors beyond your control. The truth is, much of business is a guess. That's why it's important to be able to bounce back and reenergize a team when failure strikes. Because it will.

Focus

A company-of-one leader has to become an expert at deftly saying no. You can learn to view saying no as an actual actionable strategy, as opportunities, tasks, distractions, plans, meetings, and so on all come up frequently. By saying no to anything that won't serve your business or your team, you can open up space to focus on a better opportunity in your business. You need to learn how to evaluate those options quickly and figure out which ones are good to pursue and which ones to say no to.

Decisiveness

Decision-making can be mentally taxing and draining, and when that happens, many people start to make bad decisions because they're tired of deciding. By scaling down large, stressful decisions into smaller, more digestible decisions, you can choose a direction more quickly, in a smarter way, and with less stress involved.

"EVERY DAY I'M HUSTLIN'"

While working at scaling up resilience, control, speed, and simplicity is important to leading a company of one, if you fail to approach this work with mindfulness, big problems can ensue.

There are more than 500,000 articles listed on Google about "hustling" in entrepreneurship (and none are about the Rick Ross rap song quoted in the section title). For some reason, working for yourself and pushing yourself to the limits every single day are inextricably linked — as if working more is working better. Just as we discussed in Chapter 2, more isn't better — better is better. There are advantages to putting in the time and effort to master a skill, but there's also a great need for balance. When hustling turns sleeplessness into a badge of honor and work demands push health, family, and friends to the back burner, it's definitely time to take a break.

On Apple's television show *Planet of the Apps,* one contestant admits, "I rarely get to see my kids. That's a risk you have to take." Is it really? That kind of hustling, putting work above everything else, is inconsistent with the mind-set of running a company of one — with working better instead of working more. A company of one who disagrees with this idea that workaholism is required to succeed in tech and big business alike is David Heinemeier Hansson, a Danish programmer who created the popular Ruby on Rails web framework and is a partner at the software development firm Basecamp. Hansson despises this paradigm of working more as the only way to be successful. He believes that the pressure to work more doesn't just get passed down from leadership; rather, it's amplified as it moves outward through a company. He believes that companies need to stop hustling and should encourage their employees to focus on accepting that there's life outside of work, that there's real usefulness to sleep and recuperation, and that their work habits should be much calmer.

Workaholism, a term coined in 1971 by psychologist Wayne Oates, is the epitome of hustling. The workaholic's need for work becomes so excessive that it creates disturbances in their health and relationships. Interestingly, Oates found that hustlers don't outperform nonhustlers; the only noticeable impact of their hustling is higher job stress, greater work-life conflict, and deteriorating health. His research found no relationship between workaholism and greater financial reward or self-efficacy.

Crew, a company that connects freelance designers and developers with companies that need contract work done, doesn't believe in set hours for its employees. The company doesn't expect employees to work eight hours a day, or to work between 9:00 AM and 5:00 PM. Crew lets its employees schedule work time when they are more energetic and focused—working as little or as much as they need to finish realistic tasks. Crew cares more about the work that's accomplished than about the time it takes to do it.

Do we really need to push our workers and ourselves to work longer hours to see better results? Or do we just need to get better at working the same amount or less?

The value of leading a company of one is your ability to stay agile and nimble. However, this advantage requires constant vigilance, because as success happens, opportunities happen— mostly opportunities to grow and scale up. But to stay a company of one and stick to the definition of success you've set for your-self and your leadership, you will have to turn down opportunities that aren't a good fit. Companies of one need to be relentless in what they say no to, since plans, tasks, distractions, meetings, and emails, though they may all seem productive to a team at first, can become counterproductive quickly if not well managed. In saying no to anything that doesn't fit, you leave room to say yes to those rare opportunities that do fit — opportunities that align with the values and ideas of your business.

DEBUGGING THE MYTH OF INDEFATIGABLE LEADERSHIP

Historian Henry Adams stated that power is a tumor that ends up killing its victims' sympathies. That assessment may seem quite harsh or excessive, but it's backed by both psychological and neu-roscientific studies.

Sukhvinder Obhi, a neuroscientist at McMaster University, coined the term "power paradox" to describe what happens when we gain power through leadership: we subsequently lose some of the capabilities we needed to gain it in the first place — such as empathy, self-awareness, transparency, and gratitude. Dacher Keltner, a professor of psychology at Berkeley, had similar results from his twenty years of researching the behavior of leaders — the qualities that lead to the leadership roles we achieve are the exact qualities that diminish once leadership roles are attained.

As the leader of a company of any size, you're subject to the myth that you've got to be indefatigable. Entrepreneurialism idolizes workaholism and sacrifice of anything in service to the work and the company — and puts the weight and responsibility of the entire business squarely on one person's shoulders.

That seems bleak, right? But Rand Fishkin, the onetime CEO and now "wizard" of MOZ (a company that analyzes SEO and marketing data), is very hopeful. Rand grew MOZ from a blog to a consultancy to a product business in rapid succession, and revenue grew from $300,000 in 2006 to over $48 million in 2014, with 100 percent revenue growth year after year for several years in a row. By most societal and business measures, Rand seemed to have succeeded as a leader—but no external definition of success can prevent mental illness. When Rand became depressed, he had to step down as CEO of MOZ. Through this difficult experience, however, he gained a lot of valuable insight into what it takes to lead a company, whether large or small. Much of what he learned is backed by scientific research but nevertheless runs counter to traditional business advice and the mythology of infallible leadership. Let's look at the role of empathy, self-awareness, transparency, and gratitude in growing into and, more important, maintaining a healthy leadership role.

Rand's first insight is that self-awareness is an absolute requirement. By fostering the ability to notice things about yourself—your own depression, for example—you can remove or put into remission the so-called power tumor. The more you get to know yourself, what your triggers are, and what personally drives you outside of external motivation, the more you can optimize a healthy role for yourself as a leader.

By recognizing that we are all human—and that all humans are imperfect—we can break down and debug this idea that leaders have to be infallible. As leaders, our job is to be self-aware and to check in on ourselves regularly. For Rand, that means spending thirty minutes every Friday with his wife, Geraldine, to talk openly about the worries and stresses of their week. For others, it can mean seeking external or professional help. It's crazy to assume that any one person can take on all of the stress and demands of a leadership role, and sometimes even the weight of an entire company, without having someone else to talk with and to help debug problems. This is how resilience, a major factor in building and sustaining a company of one, can be developed — by sharing the burdens as needed.

Even companies of one should never try to do everything or deal with everything alone. And even working for yourself doesn't have to mean working by yourself. As Rand says, "If therapy is good enough for Tony Soprano, it's good enough for you."

Empathy, which is a large part of Obhi's power paradox (and we'll talk even more about this in Chapter 7), is feeling *with* people, according to Dr. Brené Brown. In many quickly growing companies, however, leaders feel that they are required to detach from human relationships and focus on using people as resources to achieve necessary growth by any means necessary. The problem is that a leader who stops feeling what is either motivating or demotivating within their team stops being able to lead.

Finally, leaders need to practice gratitude. Adam Grant of Wharton found that when people take the time to thank their contractors, employees, and coworkers, they become much more engaged and productive. Even small expressions of gratitude work — like thankful emails or public recognition. Kyle at Hudl, for instance, gives out awards to the designers who have the most impact in the organization. Keltner's research illustrates that even in professional sports, players who show their appreciation through behavior like bear hugs and fist bumps with other players inspire their teammates to play better and win nearly two more games per season (which is sometimes the difference between making the playoffs or not).

So, by remaining self-aware, being open about our personal successes and failures in equal measure, empathizing with the people we work with, and expressing appreciation for them, we can work toward a cure for the "power tumors" of leadership. The glorification of indefatigable leaders is exactly the source of most problems, because their failures and flaws are ignored instead of debugged and learned from.

Here is why Rand is hopeful about leadership — all of these attributes are slowly making their way into corporate and entrepreneurial culture. Companies like Google, Facebook, General Mills, Ford, and even Goldman Sachs now have training programs that debug and work at helping with the problems that stem from leadership. There's still a long way to go, but great progress continues to be made toward a revised view of leaders as not so much the mythical heroes of modern culture as fallible humans who are just like everyone else.

BEGIN TO THINK ABOUT:

- Where you could strike a balance between autonomy and guidance
- What areas you could learn more about that would benefit your business and make you a more well-rounded generalist
- Steps you could take to strike a balance between hustlin' and recuperation

4

■

Growing a Company That Doesn't Grow

I F EXCESSIVE AND BLIND GROWTH are the main causes of business failure, then how do we start and run a business to avoid all of that?

Growth can definitely be enticing and exciting. Making more money, increasing a customer base, garnering national media attention—none of these accomplishments are inherently wrong or bad. They just need to be balanced with meaningful, long-term strategies. A lot of "growth-hacking" (a Silicon Valley term for the kind of exponential growth that tech folks salivate over) employs pushy and even sometimes shady tactics to keep growing in spite of the excessive churn that's produced.

For example, by adding a pop-up message offering access to a free report on every page on your website, you might increase the number of subscribers to your company's mailing list, but you might also end up with a list that has few email opens and more unsubscribes, making your net-net growth very low or even negative. A company of one would have a mind-set more in line with providing a great newsletter with lots of valuable content of interest to the people it wants to attract; its overall subscription rate might be lower, but the open-rate and retention would be higher.

Kate O'Neill, a consultant to *Fortune* 500 firms and an accomplished speaker, understands the type of meaningful growth that companies of one need to employ. She shows companies like Netflix and Toshiba how to use data to make customer experiences better; with this strategy, overall growth is the result of careful planning around user happiness.

Kate's superpower is being able to look at data and then apply it to the human experience. She's noticed a pattern where growth-hacking companies focus on exponential user acquisition. They prioritize attracting customers, not determining the type of customers they want or the experience they want to give people once they become customers. She has found that growth as a one-dimensional metric for success is useless in the absence of real reasons for it or ways to support customers once they're acquired. Most companies don't even need that kind of excessive growth to be profitable. Companies like Airbnb have to start with a huge inventory — Airbnb needed to amass places to stay before it could make a dent in the market — but most companies don't require so large a market share to start.

When Kate worked for Magazines.com, her role was to assume the overall strategy for acquiring customers. Previously, the strategy had been to grow right away to gain more customers, the thinking being that simply adding more customers would lead to more revenue. In looking at the collected data, however, Kate realized that user growth would cost more than user retention. By decreasing the number of subscription cancellations, Magazines.com would see better profits and gains than it would by trying to increase the number of subscribers. Since its whole business model was based on renewals, the company had to totally shift its thinking — from constantly searching for new customers to making sure existing customers were so pleased with the service that they'd renew for another year. Kate showed the company that the number of renewing customers was a far more important metric for success (and far cheaper) than the number of new customers acquired. Magazines.com also changed its home-page

messaging in order to speak to existing customers, added more renewal offers, and improved customer support for paid users.

Over and over again, Kate has seen that sacrificing customer
experience for customer acquisition doesn't work long-term and
is not a sound strategy with which to start a company.

THE FOUR REASONS GROWTH IS
DESIRED FROM THE START

It seems counterintuitive, but starting—and then staying—
small requires examining growth from the outset. If a new company of one begins by looking at why most companies grow, it can
determine whether those avenues are the correct course for it to
take. Most companies grow for four reasons: inflation, investors,
churn, and ego. By examining each, we can be ready for the decisions we'll have to make and better able to prevent social or business pressure from swaying us into doing something we don't
want to do or something that isn't right for our business.

Inflation is as close to a constant as you'll get in business. Everything eventually costs more. The five cents your grandparents
paid for a soda is not the same price that you'll pay at a vend-
ing machine today. My parents paid $50,000 for their three-bed-
room house just outside of Toronto in the early 1980s, but there's
not even a micro-condo available for that price now. So inflation
always happens, and if a business can't keep up, its profits will
shrink. The simple solution is to raise your rates each year to
keep up and then invest any extra profit in those places that pay
out higher than inflation (in other words, don't keep the bulk of
your business profits in a bank account that earns 0.001 percent
interest).

Investors, even if they own the company, are the biggest reason businesses want to grow. If a VC firm puts $1 million into
your company today, it will want to see a return at least three

times that much (and more if they're early-stage investors) within a few years. To hit those goals, growth has to be excessive. Even if you invest your own money to start a company, you'll want to see a good payoff for the risk you took. However, if you're able to start small — with little to no upfront investments — you can focus on running your business and making it better for the customers you serve instead of being constantly aware of the need to be "paid back" for what you put in.

As discussed briefly earlier, churn is what happens when existing customers decide they don't want to be customers anymore. So the revenue they generated needs to be replaced with revenue from new customers. If your churn is higher than your user acquisition rate, then you're in a downward spiral. Most of the time, companies try to fix churn, as we saw with Kate O'Neill, by focusing on adding more customers to the mix instead of working at reducing the reasons existing customers are leaving. According to the Econsultancy/Responsys Cross-Channel Marketing Report, adding a new customer costs five times as much as keeping an existing one. So while prioritizing acquisition over retention can aid growth, it's also extremely expensive. The same study found that companies are still much more likely to put their efforts into finding new customers than keeping existing ones.

Ego is the final reason most companies want to grow. It's also the trickiest, because it's harder to overcome. As a society, we give people more clout and respect if they own a large company, so building one is a desirable goal. Many of us dream of being in charge of a large company but fail to look at the bigger picture and think about the impact of such growth on our personal lives, or even on the type of work we enjoy doing. Growth adds complexity, often strains relationships, and ratchets up stress. Not all of us have a father who's got a sticky note on the family computer monitor that says, "OVERHEAD = DEATH." When we start to examine why we want to see more and more growth, we may conclude that the main reason is wanting to appear more respected than we really are. Ego is usually overcome once we determine what our reason was for starting our business in the first place.

Staying small and not focusing entirely on growth keep your own integrity and personality at the heart of the business, making it much easier to run your business or team in a way that suits you and helps customers.

As Gary Sutton, author of *Corporate Canaries,* says, "You can't sell your way out of an unprofitable business." So starting your own company of one with a focus on profitability right from the start, when you're at your leanest, is imperative. Your measuring stick for success doesn't have to be growth as a one-dimensional metric; it can be something more personal and focused on your specific company of one — like the quality of what you sell, employee happiness, customer happiness and retention, or even some greater purpose.

IN THE BEGINNING . . .

People sometimes tend to focus on the wrong things when starting a business, like office space, scaling, websites, business cards, computers. You can add expenses or bigger ideas later, once revenue is coming in. But if your idea requires a lot of money, time, or resources to start, you're probably thinking too big too soon. Scale it down to what can be done right now, on the cheap and fast, and then iterated upon.

The comedian Steve Martin has had similar thoughts about starting out and immediately focusing on the wrong things. Budding comedians have asked Martin, over and over again, "How do I find an agent?" or, "Where do I get photo headshots done?" or, "What comedy clubs should I start at?" The only question they should be asking, Martin notes, is: "How do I get really good at comedy?"

To start a company of one, you should first figure out the smallest version of your idea and then a way to make it happen quickly. Automation can happen later. Scale, if desired, can happen later. Infrastructure and process can happen later. Focus on where you can test the waters without a massive investment of time or money, and then pay attention to what happens when casual contacts turn into customers, even if it's only a handful at first. *Why did they buy? What motivated them to do so? How can I keep them happy?* And most important: *How can I help them succeed?*

To emphasize that last point, customers really don't care if you're profitable. But if what you sell them can help them become profitable, they'll never want to leave your business. They'll stay on as customers and then probably tell others to become your customers too. When you treat your relationship with your customer base as simply transactional, you'll be preoccupied with how much you can sell them and how often. The more you begin to treat new customers as real relationships that you can grow and foster, and the more you can figure out how what you do can help them, the more likely they are to want to stay on as customers. Customer success is the cornerstone of a profitable company of one.

Alexandra Franzen is the author of several books and has written for such publications as *Time, Forbes,* and *Newsweek* for the last ten years. Previously, she had a full-time job in radio broadcasting. A few days after quitting, she didn't start renting office space or buying business cards; rather, she just began emailing every single person she knew. Her parents, friends, college professors, former coworkers, internet friends . . . everyone she could think of. She wrote each one a personal email stating she had left her radio job, she was now working as a freelance writer, and she was ready for new projects.

Alex also mentioned the type of work she was looking for. By the end of the week, she had emailed sixty people, and almost everyone had written back — either giving her ideas about others to contact or asking to hire her. She began with three small projects, and those led to three more as her first clients hired her a second time for a new project or referred her to someone else who needed writing work done. It all snowballed from there, and now she's booked almost a *year* in advance. She didn't start with a vision for growth and profit or a vision of what the next several steps would be — she began with what could immediately result in paying customers. Then and only then, based on profit, did she increase her expenses (but only a little) and make some business purchases.

People often feel like they have to move away from obscurity in their new business as quickly as possible. While obscurity can equal less exposure to potential customers at the outset, starting out small and without a massive audience is perfect because it enables you to gain experience and play with your business ideas. Not to mention that there aren't many people watching if you fall flat on your face. Starting out small is the best time to learn what your business truly is and why it serves who it serves. There's no need to rush to be noticed faster than you can handle.

Starting a company of one requires that you embrace working on what's achievable now, which usually means embracing less than your vision for your ideal future. Remember, at the start you're the smallest and most agile you'll ever be. You have fewer (or no) customers, less established processes, and less name recognition. Being small and measuring meaningful growth based on profits instead of projections ensure much more stability.

We often think that we need to have everything in place — all the systems, all the automations, all the processes — to be ready to launch a digital product. We want everything all polished and perfect before we hit "publish." But most of the time this doesn't happen. Most of the time, in fact, waiting until everything is totally perfect can only hurt or delay your launch.

You can't start a business with every idea you've got for it listed in the "need to have" column. You'll never get anywhere. Plus, a lot of your assumptions about what you need might change once people start buying and using what you've made. A true "need to have" is whatever will make your idea fall apart if you don't have it. For example, if your idea is a health care SEO consultancy, your business first needs to thoroughly understand SEO and its implications for hospital websites; otherwise, your idea is of no use to hospitals. But does your consultancy need an office when working from home or in a cheaper coworking space would suffice? Does your company need glossy business cards if most of your connections are made online? Does it even need a printer if contracts and documents are all sent digitally? These are all examples of "nice to haves" that can come later, after your business is up and running.

Crew, a company we discussed in Chapter 3, started out with a single form, on a one-page website, that manually matched businesses with designers and programmers. Over time, as revenue grew, the company was able to create software and automations that helped scale the volume of matches. But at first, Crew was able to launch and test the idea of a matching service almost instantly by helping a single company get matched to the right freelancer. Scaling down an idea that you can start right now puts the focus on helping people immediately with what you have available right now and are resourceful enough to provide, like a sort of business MacGyver. If your business only has an expertise plus a figurative stick of gum, a paper clip, and a ball of twine, think: Whom can I help with these things?

In short, start small. Start with just the smallest version of your idea and a way to make it happen. Instead of waiting (sometimes for years) for bigger wins to happen, you can use small wins to propel you. That's actually a much smarter way to launch. Easing up on the "growth equals success" mentality opens you up to starting and becoming more profitable much sooner.

IF SCALE ISN'T THE GOAL, WHAT IS?

We need to reexamine our relationship with thinking big and success. Questioning growth—or at least, not scaling—isn't the same as staying static and unchanging. Even a business that doesn't want to grow much needs to constantly learn, adapt, and refine. The cost of living, labor, equipment, materials, travel— all increase year over year. Companies of one aren't anti-scale; rather, they're aware that they need to determine which areas of their business need to scale and when it makes the most sense to do so. Scale can sometimes create efficiency, and volume can increase profit margins. But without business introspection, scale and volume could be chased as vanity metrics rather than as accurate measures that determine profit.

There's a real difference between growth as a goal and growth as a direct result of profit from sales of a valuable product. Letting growth as a goal guide your company's decisions can be shortsighted or result in high churn. Whereas if your decisions are guided by growth resulting from profit, you stay focused on how you can continue to make things better for your customers —with better products, better experiences, better support, and increased success for them. This is growth that stems from doing things correctly, not from making growth your top priority and just hoping you do everything right.

In public companies on stock exchanges, there's pressure from stockholders to see stock prices increase constantly so that there's positive return on investment. The same is true for private companies with investors — they want to make a return to show those investors that investing in the company was a smart idea. The majority of companies, however, don't need to chase growth to appease outside investors. Companies of one can get by paying only an income to their owners.

Peldi Guilizzoni founded a wire-framing company called Balsamiq in 2008. Before that, he was a senior software engineer at Adobe. Balsamiq has always been privately owned, profitable, small, and focused on being better instead of bigger. Its goal — providing great software that's valuable and easy to use — leads to more customers and more profit. This approach varies from that of other software companies, which is to acquire more customers and earn greater profits that can happen only at scale and sometimes at the expense of customer satisfaction. Each year Peldi takes out $1 million personally, keeps an eighteen-month runway in the company (in case anything bad happens), and pays out the remainder to his twenty-five-employee team (which grows by only two to three people per year). He's faced pressure to grow much faster and has even been offered VC investment, but he continues to turn it down. To him, such investments, far from helping to improve his software, would just make him beholden to growing for the sake of investor ROI. He likes to make sure he has no business debts, and the only deadlines are ones that Balsamiq self-imposes. Peldi's company grows because he focuses on simply making great software.

By focusing on customer success and happiness, Peldi avoids the dangers of "thinking big" or pushing aside profit in the hope that one day margins will be huge. Even business moguls like Richard Branson started small: the entire Virgin brand began with a single magazine called *Student*. Google began as a research project at Stanford. Facebook was targeted only at Harvard undergraduates when Mark Zuckerberg started it.

For Peldi and his team at Balsamiq, focusing on better, not big-

ger, removes any pressure to take shortcuts in software development. He gets to spend his time talking to customers instead of in
board meetings or at investor pitches. Moreover, Peldi says, "I'm
Italian. Italians measure things in generations, not quarters."

If scale isn't the goal, we can strip our business and business
ideas to their essence to discover their greatest strength. This is
the view held by Yvon Chouinard, founder of Patagonia, the clothing and outdoor gear company. Having business minimalism as
its functional ideal has led Patagonia to create an ironclad guarantee for its products, which is in essence a lifetime refund/re-
placement policy. This ideal also led Chouinard to start the charity 1% for the Planet, instead of attempting to maximize and grow
sales at all costs. Patagonia even has ad campaigns telling people,
"Don't buy this jacket," and encouraging them to repair or recycle
the clothes they already have.

GROWING WITHIN AN EXISTING ORGANIZATION

In many large companies, as your career grows, you're promoted
out of doing work with your core skill set and into managing
other people with that same skill set. Since these companies operate as pyramidal hierarchies, advancement brings increasing
influence over more and more people. This can only happen if a
company continually hires more staff, since there need to be people to manage as others get promoted.

This doesn't have to be the case for organizations that operate
under a company-of-one mind-set. But then how do you advance
in your career within a company that doesn't grow, or that grows
extremely slowly? Career growth in this case happens by increasing your scope of influence and the level of your ownership; success in these two areas allows you to stay focused on your skill
set. This is how our friends at Buffer (introduced in Chapter 2)

approach career advancement—with an interesting hybrid of a pyramidal bureaucratic hierarchy and a holocracy (a completely flat organization where no one manages anyone else).

It takes even less to start a company of one within an existing organization, like a team at a corporation. Although it's not been my own path, working at a larger company does have its benefits—for instance, not having to worry, for the most part, about insurance, administrative work, or covering your expenses. And although you can sometimes gross more as a freelancer or entrepreneur, you have to take into account many expenses you wouldn't have working for a larger company, from office rent to equipment to insurance to long sales cycles (which you can't typically charge for). This is why many people opt to work as a company of one *within* an existing business, if it's set up to foster this approach or if they can get buy-in. As we'll see, there are several benefits to doing this.

Buffer has seventy-two employees, is happy at that size, and has no short-term plans to excessively grow this team. They saw that defining their scope of influence meant determining the amount of technical prowess they needed in a subject area. For example, with the goal of being able to program for Android devices, your scope of influence can start small—say, with being able to program in Java (the primary language for Android). It then grows by how much impact you can make, like a ripple. Being able to program to accomplish your tasks creates a relatively tiny ripple (you wouldn't be hired as an Android developer if you couldn't code) and grows only as you're able to influence more, for instance, by having the expertise to make sound decisions around Android for your whole team. Your scope of influence can potentially increase to become industry-wide (such as being asked to speak at Android events), your tiny ripple having turned into a massive wave.

The second factor in career growth is ownership. Ownership

is related to how Buffer assigns responsibility to each employee. Junior programmers just starting at the company are given only tasks to do, not any ownership on a project, along with responsibility for doing the work, learning, and being mentored by others. As their careers continue, they'll be able to own specific projects within their team — and be accountable for the deliverables associated with those projects. Finally, as their career advances even further, they'll be given ownership over entire disciplines within the company and all the deliverables that come from that discipline. For instance, a CTO is in charge of everything, company-wide, that relates to technology and programming.

Katie Womersley manages engineers at Buffer and helped come up with this "scope of influence" and "ownership career" framework. She's what Buffer calls a "people manager" — she's in charge of people decisions in engineering. In this model, Katie makes decisions in engineering as they relate to people, as she has a scope of influence and ownership over that entire team. But in this style of organization, an engineering team member can make specific decisions as they relate to their own scope of influence and control — for example, the team member who knows the most about Android. In this way of doing things, different people are in charge of different areas. So it's possible to have a scenario where two employees are working together and one is in charge of one type of programming and the other is subordinate, but in an HR scenario their roles are reversed. Basically, the most qualified and best-suited person makes the decisions for each specific project.

Buffer's goal in organizing the company this way is to illustrate that there's no ceiling for rising: employees who don't want to outgrow their jobs don't have to. An employee who loves programming for Android can simply acquire more and more Android-related ownership and decision-making abilities. Other employees may choose to grow to manage Android projects, or to become people managers. Buffer employees never have to choose between stagnation and leading people — they can choose to go deeper into their area of expertise or go wider by building a name for themselves outside the company in their area of expertise (which is then rewarded).

This is exactly how you grow within a large company of one or how a large organization can operate more like a company of one.

BEGIN TO THINK ABOUT:

- How you could prioritize your existing customers or transform them into repeat customers
- The smallest version of your business idea that you could start with now, with little to no investment
- How you want to grow as a business, or as an employee who doesn't require transitioning into work you don't actually want to do

PART II

Define

5

∎

Determining the
Right Mind-Set

REGARDLESS OF WHETHER OR NOT your company of
one is just you or is part of a larger organization, with
greater autonomy comes greater responsibility to do the
work expected of you. How you think about work is important to
how work gets done.

To succeed as a company of one, you have to have a real underlying purpose. Your *why* matters as an unseen but ever-pres-
ent element that drives your business. Your purpose is more than
just a pretty-sounding mission statement on your website; it's
how your business acts and represents itself. And it's what your
business sometimes places above even profit.

As more and more consumers are making purchases related
to shared value (even over price), companies are responding by
aligning their true purpose with how they act at every step along
the supply chain, how they market to and pitch potential customers, and even how they support their products and services.
Companies of one recognize that economic value and shared pur-
poses don't have to be mutually exclusive — they can drive sales
and also ensure sustainability.

Yvon Chouinard, the founder of Patagonia, believes that much
of his company's success is due to being a "responsible" company.
A shared set of values around environmental stewardship and

sustainability guides how they do business, from how they hire and train employees to why they've had on-site day care since they started, to why they cofounded the charity 1% for the Planet. This approach may run counter to how a lot of clothing companies operate, but Patagonia's purpose is to produce less clothing, to make it last longer, and to offset its price socially and environmentally. Because this purpose resonates with Patagonia's audience, they're able to charge a higher price for their responsible clothing. Furthermore, the top five companies in 1% for the Planet saw record sales years during the 2008–2009 recession, when most other companies were losing money. In a thriving economy people gladly buy products that align with their values, and in a downturn they spend less and do business with companies they respect and trust. So either way, having a purpose is a win.

Seventh Generation is another business that's built around purpose — so much so that the purpose is part of their name: they consider the impact every product they create will have on the next seven generations. This purpose has guided them to create plant-based, nontoxic cleaning supplies and to become a B-corporation (B-corps are certified through rigorous standards of social and environmental performance, accountability, and transparency). This purpose is beneficial in several ways for Seventh Generation: They attract a younger workforce, none of whom probably thought, *Hey, I'd like to work for a household goods company when I graduate!* They also build traction through word of mouth for a market that most people wouldn't otherwise talk about. Their purpose is seen through their actions, not just their marketing efforts — they encourage both employees and customers to line-dry clothes, even at the risk of slowing sales of their dryer sheet product. Seventh Generation's purpose doesn't just result in customers feeling good about their products — it also generates approximately $250 million in revenue. In 2016, Unilever purchased Seventh Generation, which hopefully will stay true to its purpose.

Your purpose is the lens through which you filter all your business decisions, from the tiny to the monumental. We're talking about who you work with, what you offer, where you focus your time and energy, and even how you define your audience. Determining the unique purpose that underpins your company of one isn't always a quick or easy process, and there's no spreadsheet that can crunch some numbers and spit out the answer. Figuring out your purpose requires actual reflection on both your own desires and the audience you want to serve. After all, doing business boils down to serving others in a mutually beneficial way. Customers give you money, gratitude, and a shared passion, and you address their problems by applying your unique skills and knowledge to what you sell them.

Virgin founder Richard Branson summed up purpose nicely: "Success in business is no longer just about making money or moving up the corporate ladder. More and more, one of the biggest indicators of success is purpose."

If your business is fully aligned with your purpose, you'll be more motivated to keep at it, even during the tough moments; your workforce will turn over less, since employees won't have to leave their values at home when they head to work; and your customers will become and remain loyal. Your purpose will also serve as a litmus test for all your business decisions, enabling you to make smart, prompt, and more confident choices in all areas of your work.

What happens if you build your business without ever thinking about your purpose? What if you'd rather focus exclusively on acquisition and higher profits? Those activities can definitely seem more rewarding. But the more we busy ourselves with work and fail to consider why we're doing it in the first place, the more likely we are to realize (often far too late) that we're not enjoying

what we've worked so hard to build. And if you're the one building your own company of one, you're the one who has to rebuild
and change it when things don't work. It's so much easier to first
clarify your purpose, even with just a quick check-in, to make
sure it aligns (or still aligns) with where your business is heading.

John Kotter and James Heskett report in their book *Corporate
Culture and Performance* that purpose-based, values-driven companies outperform their counterparts in stock price by a factor of
twelve. They have found that, without a purpose, management
has a harder time rallying employees to increase productivity
and customers have a harder time connecting to the company.
Their decade-long research shows that purpose creates positive
outcomes far greater than the sum of its parts.

Whether you're a *Fortune* 500 CEO or a freelancer, your purpose is what drives you to succeed and defines what success is.
It's not so much what you do as how and why you do it. Your purpose is your values put into action. For example, CVS stopped
selling tobacco products because cigarettes — previously worth
billions in revenue to the pharmacy chain — didn't align with its
purpose of helping people on their path to better health.

Defining your purpose has more to do with your personal values and ethics than with business plans or marketing strategies.
You can't fake your purpose. Your gut and your customers simply won't let you. And really, why would you want to? You'll get so
much more enjoyment and satisfaction from running your business in alignment with your purpose. If you don't feel a deep connection to your purpose, no one else will feel it either.

Not having a purpose runs counter to how a company of one
should operate because a lack of purpose will keep you focused
on short-term gains over long-term sustainability. By assuming
that quarterly growth in profits is the only factor in your success,
you risk overlooking the well-being and success of your customer
base (which, we learned from the last chapter, happens at your

own peril). "Growth and scale at all costs" is a broken, outdated, and unsubstantiated model that disregards what research has told us about the hazards of growth and scale.

Given the success of Patagonia, Seventh Generation, and many other such organizations, it's clear that purpose isn't just a fluffy, new-age paradigm for businesses uninterested in profit. A study done by Michael Porter, a Harvard Business School professor, and Mark Kramer, the cofounder of the social-impact firm FSG, found that taking a "shared value" approach to purpose generates positive economic impacts for companies. They can align their business with their values and with what matters to their customers by reconsidering how they produce and sell products and redefining what productivity means for employees (valuing their rest and happiness and discouraging overworking).

A well-integrated, shared purpose lets a company of one set its true direction, leading to easier decision-making, higher retention of team members, and greater connection to customers.

WHEN PASSION IS A PROBLEM

Purpose and passion are quite different.

While purpose is based on a core set of values held by a company or even a business owner and shared with customers, passion is simply a whim based on what we think we enjoy doing. The tired business advice that we should all "follow our passion" implies that we are entitled to getting paid to do work that is always enjoyable.

A well-cited 2003 study of college students at the University of Quebec by Robert Vallerand found that they were more passionate about sports, arts, and music than anything they were studying. Unfortunately, only 3 percent of all jobs can be found in the sports, music, and art industries. And just because you're passionate about, say, tennis doesn't mean you can become the next

Serena Williams, no matter how hard you try. "Follow your passion" is irresponsible business advice.

Barbara Córcoran, a real estate investor and a "shark" on the popular television show *Shark Tank,* said that she didn't follow her passion; instead, she discovered it by accident as she worked her ass off. Her passion came *after* her hard work — as a result of it — not the other way around. Known for her shrewd pragmatism on the show, Corcoran says that it's more important to focus on solving problems than on passion. Her problem-solving focus allows her to better evaluate new business ventures that are presented to her on the show.

When you focus on solving problems or on making a difference, passion may follow, because you're actually involved in the work you're doing instead of just dreaming that you might be passionate about something. Cal Newport, the best-selling author of *So Good They Can't Ignore You,* argues that passion is the side effect of mastery. To Newport, following your passion is fundamentally flawed as a career strategy because it fails to describe how most successful people ended up with compelling careers and can lead to chronic job-shifting and angst when your reality falls short of your passionate dream for your career. Newport believes that we need to be craftspeople, focused on getting better and better at how we use our skills, in order to be valuable to our company and its customers. The craftsperson mind-set keeps you focused on what you can offer the world; the passion mind-set focuses instead on what the world can offer you.

Too many people assume that meaningful work or ideas are the result of passion. Research from William MacAskill of Oxford University has shown that engaging work helps you develop passion, not the other way around. This kind of work draws you in, holds your attention, and gives you a sense of flow (being absorbed in the work and losing track of time). Engaging work comprises four key components: clearly defined assignments, tasks you excel at, performance feedback, and work autonomy.

All this being said, countless books, bloggers, and business leaders will continue to tell you that the key ingredient to a happy, meaningful life is to find the courage to follow your passion. This call is alluring, especially when it seems like others have simply packed up their nine-to-five lives, jumped headfirst into their passions, and ended up thriving.

But what I've noticed is that there are two key ingredients that most successful businesspeople don't talk about when they're giving keynote speeches about how smart they were to make their leap into a more passion-filled work life. The first is that they were skilled at what they did *before* they took a leap — so skilled that they were doing well enough that if their leap to something new faltered, they'd still be okay. Not to mention that what they leaped to was completely built off the skills they were currently using and that were already in demand. The second missing ingredient in their account of successfully "following their passion" is that they were able to test their leap with a smaller jump before they climbed to the top of the highest platform. Most of these speakers neglect to mention that they didn't just willy-nilly jump; rather, they did a small jump first to make sure they could land it (that is, they made sure there was enough demand for their offerings) and not drown once they hit the water.

Looking at my own career, I can say that I've succeeded in changing the type of work I've done over the last twenty years only when those two key ingredients were present.

I started my own business doing web design only after I became an in-demand designer at an agency. I built up the skills as an employee until the clients of that agency wanted to leave with me when I quit. If I hadn't done that, I wouldn't have even started working for myself. (I did so only because clients called after I quit, wanting to bring their business to wherever I had moved.) In fact, I wasn't passionate about web design, or even passionate about starting my own business. I found the courage to do it only because I had a small list of companies that wanted to pay me from day one.

When I started selling online courses, the same elements were present. I used the skills I had built for years as a designer to make courses on related subjects. And before I moved entirely into products, I spent a few years transitioning, waiting until I was sure that selling these online products would make me enough money before completely diving in.

On the other hand, when I first tried back in the 1990s to pivot into business consulting without having any related, built-up skills, I had almost no bites from clients. I was young (and naive) and thought that since I had helped design a handful of websites, I understood how all businesses everywhere work. Consulting seemed far more fun than just designing websites, so I found the courage to start promoting that as a service. The problem was that I was only just starting my journey as a designer and hadn't come close to building up the necessary skills to consult for other businesses.

In short, my business skills weren't in demand at all back then, and I had never even tested them to see if anyone would pay for them before spending a ton of time updating my website to promote them. Doing well with business consulting didn't happen until I had years of experience under my belt — both by working with clients and by running my own companies.

The same thing happened when I tried to pivot into something I was passionate about without testing to see whether there was any demand. Years ago, I started not one but two software companies. Yes, I was the designer for them, which was a skill I had built up and created demand for, but I started both companies without first determining whether they'd be financially viable. I worked for months and months with partners to create products that we hadn't even come close to demonstrating anyone would be willing to pay for. Both companies ultimately — and spectacularly — failed.

I didn't start out with a passion to be a web designer, a writer, or an online course creator. I didn't even have the courage to jump headfirst into those jobs. They happened slowly after I honed my related skills to the point where they were in demand. The passion for those jobs followed, but only once I had spent a lot of time doing them and getting better at them. And then I moved fully into them once I could prove (mostly to myself) that they would pay. In contrast, when I tried to be a consultant in my early twenties and when I tried to start two software companies, I failed completely because I hadn't yet honed the skills required for those endeavors — plus those skills were definitely not in demand and I couldn't demonstrate that even a single person would pay for them.

Of course, "courage" and "passion" sound better and more romantic than "skills" and "viability tests." Courage and passion can be great if you want to skydive or take up a hobby like playing the ukulele. But when it's your livelihood at stake, being courageous and following your passion should take a backseat to using the skills that you can build up and validate with revenue.

This might seem like a downer of a message, but it's not. Thankfully, you don't have to waste time trying to figure out what you're passionate about or hoping that one day you find the courage inside yourself to leap into your passion full-time. Passion and courage are almost impossible to control and can easily leave you feeling bad about yourself. It's far easier to simply work at getting really good at something in demand, discovering how those skills can be applied to something else, and then testing your idea in a small way to see if it will pay.

Another study on college students, from psychologist Jeffrey

Arnett, found that most postgrads expect the work they do in their career to not be just a job but an adventure. The problem is that most of the subjects felt entitled to meaningful and adventurous work, but no obligation to put in the time and effort to master the skill set required. Just as autonomy is achieved through mastery of skills and ownership of an ability to solve problems, so too is passion. Passion doesn't precede mastery, but follows it.

The feeling among some employees, team members, or even business owners that they are owed something just for showing up is a difficult pill to swallow. Linda Haines, who ran a human resources department at a large international company, says that many people who were raised to feel like they're always winners, regardless of their relative efforts, merits, or skills, feel entitled to promotions and advances just because they show up to the office. The downside to this feeling of entitlement is that it leads to problems within teams and in dealing with customers, manifesting as resistance to feedback, overestimation of talents and accomplishments, little sense of team loyalty or loyalty to a purpose, and a tendency to blame others, even customers, for mistakes. Entitled business owners and workers have a hard time adapting to challenging situations, which is the opposite of the company-of-one trait of resilience.

Engaging work, not entitled work, can be anything from collecting garbage to serving coffee, to coaching billionaires, to becoming a company of one inside a large organization. That's it. While no one should ever tell us to not pursue our passions, we can't feel simply entitled to make money from them. If you're engaged by your work — for the independence it allows, for the sense of completion when you're done, for its contribution to making the world a better place — passion is likely to follow. Passion isn't the catalyst that creates success, but more often what develops *after* success is achieved. Taking action and doing work, as a first step, create momentum, and this momentum happens when you're caught up in — and enjoying — the process of your work, not its possible outcomes.

The gist is this: you can pursue any passion you want, but you shouldn't feel entitled to make money off it. Passion in work comes from first crafting a valuable skill set and mastering your work. This is great news, because it means you no longer have to beat yourself up for not finding your true, hidden passions. Instead, you can simply get to work.

THE TRUE COST OF OPPORTUNITIES

The final part of aligning your mind-set with a company-of-one mentality is learning to handle the onslaught and weight of opportunities and obligations.

Just as growth in revenue and employees should be questioned as to whether or not it will make things better or simply bigger, we must also question the idea that a busier life, with a packed schedule, is a better life.

Opportunities are just obligations wearing an appealing mask. There might be a positive outcome to seizing them, but they always come at a cost — in terms of time, attention, or resources. No matter how hard you try, you can't scale the amount of time in your day. And since you can't somehow buy more hours, you need to find ways to use those hours better.

Curiously, up until the 1950s, the word "priority" was almost always singular in use — it wasn't until later that the misguided belief that multitasking is a good idea took hold, along with "priorities" (plural). We now incorrectly assume that we must have numerous priorities and multitask to get ahead in business, even though working this way can deeply affect (and hurt) our productivity. With a key trait of a company of one being the speed at which things can happen and be accomplished, productivity is required. A Microsoft Research study found that attempting to focus on more than one priority at a time reduces productivity by as much as 40 percent, which is the cognitive equivalent of pulling an all-nighter. Research done by Hewlett-Packard found that the IQs of employees who were interrupted by email, calls, or messaging were reduced by more than ten points—which is twice the impact of smoking marijuana.

Jocelyn Glei, the best-selling author of *Unsubscribe,* is obsessed with avoiding distraction to do more work that matters. She works for herself now; previously she was the founding editor and director of *99U,* so she's experienced both leading an autonomous team and leading herself. In terms of productivity, she believes that the main difference is motivation and momentum. Working on a high-functioning team, you're naturally playing off other members to accomplish your piece of a project, and that keeps you wanting to move things forward by focusing on your part. When you are a company of one without a team or employees, you have to generate your own momentum and motivation to get work done. It's up to you to set your schedule, manage obligations, and avoid distractions.

Companies of one need to become adept at "single-tasking"— doing one thing for an extended period of time without distraction. This capacity helps you focus on the right tasks, do them faster, and do them with less stress. Gloria Mark, a professor in the Department of Informatics at the University of California, found that for every interruption, it takes an average of twenty-three minutes and fifteen seconds to fully get back to the task. Fewer distractions means speedier work.

Many large organizations have changed how they run fairly recently by adopting the startup ethos of flatter hierarchies, open workspace, multiple projects for every team member, and even asynchronous communication (like Slack). In these workplaces, employees no longer feel like they have one singular task to perform in their jobs, and they have to self-manage many of their responsibilities and their time. Even though these traits are part of being a company of one inside a larger organization, we need to unpack what it means to develop this autonomy and how best to do so.

To manage yourself within a larger team, you have to become adept at articulating your workload to other people. There may be several team members, and even multiple managers, vying for space in your workday. Even when you work for yourself, multiple clients or customers will be simultaneously requiring your attention. If you handle these demands poorly, you'll become overworked, stressed out, and unable to perform. Handling them well requires constant vigilance and an ability to communicate to others the consequences of taking time away from customers for things like new projects, meetings, conference calls, and reports.

Glei believes that even though there are no perfect answers here, you have to be relentless in protecting your own schedule and workload. If you don't have full control over your own schedule — if, for instance, someone is telling you what to do in your job — you have to be able to explain what's currently filling your schedule and what tasks or responsibilities would need to be removed to make space for other demands. You also need to account for each day's busywork, which can eat up more time than you think. With hundreds of emails and thousands of Slack messages to answer, as well as five different managers to report to, you can be left with very little time to do your core work. So articulating to people requesting your time what you can and cannot do becomes key. A daily meeting can't fit into a schedule that's already full. Making yourself available eight hours a day on a chat leaves you no time to do focused, deep work.

Since most of us aren't even aware of how much time daily job maintenance takes up, Glei suggests doing a productivity audit once or twice a year: for a week or two, record what tasks you're working on, for how long, and where the big distractions lie. With this record, you can reapportion your time more appropriately or even create a "stop doing" list—such as stay off social media, forgo daily meetings, or be available on a chat for one hour instead of eight.

Jason Fried, a cofounder of Basecamp and author of the bestseller *ReWork,* says that it's a manager's job to protect the team's time and attention. Many corporate workers end up putting in sixty- to seventy-hour weeks because so much of the standard forty hours is taken up by interruptions. Fried believes that the norm should be every employee having a full eight hours per day of uninterrupted work to themselves. Companies and managers should demand very little of that time, and when they do, they should be required to ask for it, without the expectation of an immediate response unless it's a major emergency (for example, the servers for the company software going down).

By keeping meetings and interruptions to an absolute minimum, Fried has found that his staff enjoy their work more, can be more thoughtful about it, and spend more of their time solving problems that matter to the company. This leads to less churn and less training of new employees (since it's rarely needed) and even improves his business's bottom line by raising profits each year.

Basecamp also doesn't allow calendar sharing between employees at any level. Shared calendars can easily be abused by those who assume that others have time if there's nothing on their calendar. In fact, blank time has probably been left on their calendar so they can focus on their work.

As a company of one, it's easy to mentally beat yourself up for not accomplishing enough during a day. But how often do you take into account how rare it is, between doing your core work and managing your business, to have a full day, every day, to sit and work without interruptions? You may be failing to realize how much of your schedule is taken up with maintenance work or communication.

To combat this, I take several months off from interviews, calls, and meetings each year to create new products or write books without interruption. Being engaged in deep and focused work, because I've cut myself off from communication and availability to others, creates efficiency. Also, batching similar tasks allows me to do more work in less time. For example, I don't communicate with others — no meetings, calls, interviews, or social media — on Mondays and Fridays so I can write (words or code); I do most of my calls on Thursdays. In this way, I don't feel bad if all I do on a Thursday is meetings and interviews, because that's my singular focus for that day. I also rarely work for more than an hour on weekends, so I can recharge and enjoy a life outside of work.

Creating the image of busyness may be all the rage in startup and corporate culture, but the busier we are, the less space we have to think and be creative in solving the problems that companies of one need to solve. The Harvard economist Sendhil Mullainathan and the Princeton psychologist Eldar Shafir, authors of the book *Scarcity*, have concluded that we make bad decisions when we are strapped for time, too busy to think, and struggling to manage our obligations. Even if we take only a few hours a week of unplanned time, we can develop a bigger-picture focus or strategies for how our business actually runs.

Prior to the industrial revolution, work took up all waking hours. Everyone was either sleeping, eating, or working. The automaker Henry Ford instituted eight-hour shifts in his factory in 1914. An early advocate for breaking the day into thirds (work, sleep, family), he did so not so much out of unbridled generosity, but because he realized (so the story goes) that his workers needed free time to go out and buy more consumer goods. After many companies followed suit, we ended up with the traditional idea that work should take forty hours a week. The funny thing, though, is that any task will take up the time we give it. So if we give ourselves eight hours to work each day, our work will take eight hours, and if our tasks take less time than that, we usually fill much of the "extra" time with busywork. If we reframe the question of how we spend our time, however, we can start to figure out how long each of our tasks actually takes. Perhaps we need only four hours a day to get our work done.

As a company of one that achieves ownership over your schedule and how long you allow yourself to work, you can be overloaded with the sheer number of tasks you need to do to keep your businesses running. Researcher John Pencavel from Stanford University says that if you start to define your productivity in physical terms, you can see that your ability to focus drastically diminishes after fifty-five hours a week. So adding anything more to your schedule that takes longer will not be productive. The social badge of honor for always being busy and always working has no rewards past bragging rights. It also has no place in the company-of-one mind-set. What you should be bragging about is figuring out how to get your work done quicker and more productively.

Just as company growth should be questioned, so too should a busy schedule. How many opportunities do we really need to say yes to? Often, piling on work to get ahead comes at the price of our health, our relationships, and even our productivity. Perhaps we need to determine what "enough" is for our particular schedule and then ruthlessly stick to and defend that.

BEGIN TO THINK ABOUT:

- The true purpose of your business and whether it shows up in your actions (not just in your marketing material)

- What you are skilled at that is already in demand and where else that skill could be leveraged
- Where you could test your leap into something in a small way first
- How you could align your day/schedule to be focused on single-tasking

6

■

Personality Matters

I N HIGH SCHOOL, I WAS the kid everyone picked on. Day after day I'd get made fun of or someone would lure me into a fight. I figured my personality was the weakest part of who I was and attempted to hide it as much as I could.

It wasn't until years later—when I sent a survey to more than 10,000 customers asking why they bought my products—that I realized that my personality was the number-one factor in their decision to purchase from my business and not from someone else. As much as they wanted to buy the products I was selling, they wanted to buy them from me in particular, even if similar products were offered elsewhere or at a lower price.

What changed? My personality didn't. I'm still an awkward and excitable nerd, just like I was in high school. What did change was that I gradually became okay with sharing who I am and using my differences strategically. Once who I am became part of how I marketed and sold, more people started to respond to that. Not everyone, of course, but enough people started paying attention to my work and became customers. They liked that I was an awkward geek. They trusted me because of my personality, since a lot of them were awkward and excitable nerds too.

Personality—the authentic you that traditional business has

taught you to suppress under the guise of "professionalism" —
can be your biggest edge over the competition when you're a company of one. What's even better is that while skills and expertise
can be replicated, it's damn near impossible to replicate someone's personality and style. Especially in a company of one, where
you aren't the largest player in your niche and probably not the
cheapest, using your quirks and standing for something can be
exactly how and why you gain customers' attention.

A personality is required for your company of one, regardless
of size. Your human characteristics are the way your brand speaks
and behaves. For example, Harley-Davidson is a brand that con-
notes rebelliousness, while Snapchat is associated with being
young and fresh (although calling it "young and fresh" probably
means that I'm neither). If you don't think about the personality
of your business, your audience will assign one to you — because
people relate to other people, and your audience wants to relate to
your brand when they see it.

As a company of one, your brand should very much represent
some distinct aspect of yourself, while taking into account whom
you're trying to reach. Marie Forleo, founder of Marie Forleo International, runs an eight-figure business training company with
her distinct personality front and center. In the beginning, she
worried about being her quirky self in videos and writing because
at the time that wasn't seen as the norm in the business world,
or even in the world of other leaders she aspired to connect with,
like Oprah. Funnily enough, though, it was specifically her quirky
self that her audience related to so strongly, and when her platform grew to reach more than 250,000 subscribers in 193 countries, not only did she appear on *Oprah,* but Oprah named her a
leader for the next generation.

What do you want your brand to exude? Toughness? Sophisti-
cation? Excitement? Sincerity? Luxury? Competence?

Rand Fishkin says that newly formed companies tend to inherit the personality of their founders internally, and then externally. So personality even creates and affects company culture.

Charlie Bickford, founder of Excalibur Screwbolts, a small British manufacturer, has found that keeping his business small makes it easier to show both his staff and customers his commitment to quality and personal service. Charlie still answers customer phone lines at age seventy-four. By keeping his company small, he maintains its integrity and also places his own unique personality in front of his brand; meanwhile, his massive competitors are racing to win market share. Excalibur has endured — even after the entire industry copied his bolt-fixing techniques — by focusing on building a brand personality based on personal contact and great service. These key factors have allowed Charlie to do well at a small size and landed him an impressive range of projects, from the Olympic stadium in Atlanta to the Gottard tunnel in Switzerland.

Brand personality needs to foster a two-sided relationship — one focused on not just how your businesses can benefit or gain something from others, but on how others can benefit from having a relationship with your business. And don't confuse the personality of your brand with "acting the part" — instead, the idea is to showcase those aspects of who you naturally are as they relate to building fascination with your intended audience. Charlie, for example, has always been focused on creating products of true quality, so his company works hard to showcase that aspect of its personality.

THE ATTENTION ECONOMY

Steve Rubel, a public relations expert in New York City, says that attention is the most important currency anyone can give a business, and that attention is worth more than revenue or possessions. In an age of information — almost every piece of knowledge in the world is immediately available on computers we keep in our pockets — the vastness of what's available to learn, read, listen to, or watch causes a scarcity of attention. Every business everywhere wants a piece of this attention, both online and off.

The new "attention-as-currency" may stem from how the world has changed since the industrial revolution, which had led to sellers making all the rules. Now buyers dictate what they want, how they want it, and when. And if they aren't happy with one seller, they simply take to the internet and post their dissatisfaction, sometimes with reach greater than the seller's. For example, when blogger Amber Karnes tweeted that Urban Outfitters stole a design of an independent visual artist, her comment was quickly retweeted by other accounts with a total reach of 1.3 million followers, and then subsequently picked up by the *Huffington Post*, causing Urban Outfitters to lose 17,000 followers within hours (and no doubt having a lasting negative impact on its brand). As we'll also see in Chapter 10, attention can be instantly lost when trust is broken.

Our own minds are not always focused on our current tasks and can wander 46.9 percent of the time, according to research from Daniel Gilbert and Matthew Killingsworth, who studied 5,000 participants across eighty-three countries of ranging ages and socioeconomic status. If we ourselves rarely pay full attention to what we do, how can a business hope to gain attention long enough to convert a person into a customer? Or even have that person simply notice their business?

In other words, how can companies of one, operating with the idea that less can be better, grab the attention required to profit and thrive?

According to best-selling business author Sally Hogshead, the answer lies in developing fascination — an intense captivation and focus on a person or business. Her research on this subject, published in fourteen languages, involved more than 125,000 participants over ten years. What Sally has looked at is how businesses and people can leverage attention over others. By measuring how the world sees us, she's been able to determine how we can be fascinating to our ideal customers.

Sally contends that the key is to unlearn being boring. That is, you need to learn how to elicit a strong emotional response to your business, and the personality of your brand, because while it's easy to forget or lose interest in information, it's much harder to forget strong emotion. You can do this by allowing your business to have some aspect of your own innate personality or quirks. Fascination in a product or service builds an emotional connection, and emotional connections hold attention.

As a result of her research, Sally has compiled a twenty-eight-question personality test that, instead of explaining how you see yourself, explains how the world sees you. When I took the test, for academic curiosity's sake, the results showed that I'm a "Provocateur." This seems correct and in line with how I showcase my own brand's personality: I dislike authority and the status quo and enjoy trying new contrarian business ideas. This personality bleeds through in my writing, my sales pages for products, and even when I'm interviewed for podcasts. So I build fascination in my own audience by leaning on provoking others with ideas.

In an interview Sally did with Marie Forleo, she spoke about the tendency of large companies to be the vanilla ice cream of their market — they project a personality that's universally acceptable, but bland. For a company of one, being vanilla isn't going to allow you or your work to stand out. Companies of one have to be the pistachio ice cream of their market. For better or worse, people either absolutely love pistachio or can't stand its flavor and weird green color. For its loyal fans, pistachio ice cream stands out, demands attention, and charges a premium. Just like Excalibur Screwbolts does with its products. Just like Marie using her personality to captivate audiences in her videos with lots of chair dancing and funny stories. These are all examples of gaining attention by using and featuring personality, not by shying away from it.

Fascination is the response when you take what makes you interesting, unique, quirky, and different and communicate it. When you start to understand how the world sees your business, you can amplify that understanding by featuring the specific traits that make you, you. When you own and harness aspects of your personality strategically, you can use them as a competitive advantage in a crowded marketplace — like an artisanal bucket of pistachio ice cream that people will gladly pay $25 for (instead of going with the $4 tub of vanilla).

Don't just ask consumers to pay attention to your business. Instead, start doing the kinds of unique and unusual things that attract attention in order to make your business distinct.

NEUTRALITY CAN BE COSTLY

It can be scary to draw that line in the sand — especially when it's your business and livelihood. Doing so immediately alienates certain people or entire groups. But taking a stand is important because you become a beacon for those individuals who are your people, your tribe, and your audience. When you hoist your viewpoint up like a flag, people know where to find you; it becomes a rallying point. Displaying your perspective lets prospective (and current) customers know that you don't just sell your products or services. *You do it for a specific reason.*

The best marketing is never just about selling a product or service, but about taking a stand — showing an audience why they should believe in what you're marketing enough to want it at any cost, simply because they agree with what you're doing. Products can be changed or adjusted if they aren't functioning, but rallying points align with the values and meaning behind what you do. These bold statements are impossible to ignore and make clear that your work is more than the work, that you have a serious reason for doing it in the first place.

Derek Sivers, the former CEO of CDBaby, says that we should proudly exclude people, because we can't please everyone. That way, when someone hears our message directed specifically at them and no one else, they'll be drawn toward our message (and will pay attention). It's like creating messaging for pistachio ice cream lovers while poking fun at boring vanilla.

Tom Fishburne, from Chapter 1, says that there's power in polarization. If we try to appeal to everyone, we won't appeal to anyone in particular, muddying our message. Creating indifference or simply being another boring small company in a crowded marketplace just won't serve you well as a company of one.

The "poster child" for polarization is Marmite, the classic yeast food spread from the United Kingdom. Marmite's tagline is "You either love it or hate it," a message it's been tapping successfully for twenty years.

Guy Kawasaki, the well-known marketing specialist and venture capitalist, also thinks that we shouldn't be afraid of polarization. Large companies search for the "Holy Grail" of products that appeal to every demographic, socioeconomic background, and geographical location, but this "one size fits all" approach rarely works and often leads to mediocrity (and vanilla ice cream). Instead, Kawasaki believes, we should create products that make specifically identified groups of people very happy and ignore everyone else. The worst-case scenario is inciting no passionate reactions from anyone — no one caring enough about a product to talk about it at all, either positively or negatively.

The idea that we should be able to infinitely scale attention for what we create to everyone can quickly become our downfall —

the same kind of downfall waiting for those startups that attempt to infinitely scale customers and staff much too quickly. Expanding too quickly and for too large an audience often spells doom.

Being unique, different, and unusual can have a polarizing effect on your potential audience. But that isn't always bad.

Just Mayo, a product from the company Hampton Creek, is very polarizing, even though it's "just" mayonnaise. It's been getting a swath of media attention from lawsuits, SEC investigations, lobbying efforts, and even CEO death threats — making it even more popular to both fans and investors alike.

Just Mayo is mayonnaise without eggs. Its egglessness was why big-food behemoth Unilever, makers of Hellmann's Mayo, sued Hampton Creek, alleging false advertising because its product didn't contain eggs, an ingredient "required" for mayonnaise according to the Food and Drug Administration legal definition. (The fact that there's a government agency that defines legal ingredients for condiments is also baffling.) Unilever sued because it was losing a sizable market share to this much smaller and nimbler startup. There were also unsigned and fraudulent letters to major retailers that carried Just Mayo, alleging that the prod uct contained salmonella and listeria, in response, Target pulled Just Mayo from its shelves. The FDA cleared the company and said that those claims were unsubstantiated. But the controversy didn't end with lawsuits and letters: the American Egg Board and the U.S. Department of Agriculture began conspiring to hire journalists to denigrate Just Mayo and its CEO, Joshua Tetrick. This campaign climaxed with this statement from a now-public-record email exchange: "Can we pool our money to put a hit on him?"

By being polarizing with its eggless mayonnaise, Hampton Creek disrupted the entire mayonnaise industry. The ensuing controversy and legal battle only made its brand more desirable to its audience. In the end, Unilever not only dropped the lawsuit but, in a huge about-face, launched its own certified vegan, eggless "mayo" a few years later.

To be a polarizing company of one, you can look to three strategies. The first is *placation*: trying to change the minds of the so-called haters, those individuals who don't like your product. General Mills did this in 2008 by creating low-carb and gluten-free cake mixes, amid rising concerns over obesity and gluten sensitivities. Within three years, the number of customers who vocally disliked their mixes had dropped significantly. The second strategy is *prodding*: by intentionally antagonizing haters, you may sway neutral customers into becoming supporters if they agree with your polarizing stance. Finally, the third strategy is *amplification*: singling out a characteristic and leaning heavily on it. Marmite, already polarizing in its "love it or hate it" stance, released Marmite XO, an extra-strength version of the flavor. The company invited thirty of its best customers (found through social media) to a tasting and set up a Facebook group for the event. The promotion gleaned over 50,000 visits to the company website and over 300,000 Facebook page views. Marmite XO sold out quickly after reaching shelves.

WestJet, a highly successful Canadian airline, has taken direct aim at United Airlines' troubles with overbooking, which were highlighted when a video of a United passenger being dragged off a flight went viral. WestJet's latest marketing campaign is simply "We don't overbook," complete with the hashtag *#OwnersCare*. (WestJet brags that its passengers are all technically owners of the airline.) Memorable stories are often driven by a protagonist fighting against an antagonist, giving the audience someone to root for and to root against. After all, there's no *Star Wars* without Darth Vader. The same can occur in business: since our brains are wired for relating to and remembering good stories and epic struggles, a company that isn't telling a compelling story can devolve into boring and forgettable vanilla ice cream.

As a small business or one that isn't aiming to grow rapidly, you can use polarization to provide an avenue for reaching your potential audience — without massive advertising spends or paid user acquisition — by getting people talking. Think back to before Apple was a monolith in the tech industry, when it was a tiny company going up against the giant IBM. In a now-famous Apple television advertisement — an homage to George Orwell's classic book 1984 — a hero battles against conformity and "Big Brother." The ad was so controversial and different from all the other ads at the time that all the cable news outlets picked it up after it first aired and re-aired it for free as a news story. By being different, Apple ended up selling $3.5 million worth of its new Macintoshes just after the ad first ran.

In my own business, the stance I take on business and even social issues puts some people off. For every email I send to my weekly newsletter, I get a handful of critical replies, ranging from the standard internet vitriol to comments such as "I don't want to buy anything from you because you believe in [fill in the blank]." This is actually a good thing, as I don't want to have customers who are so angry or who complain so readily; if they paid for one of my products, I'd have to offer them technical or customer support. Their opting out of what I have to say and never buying anything from me is a win-win. When I get an email along those lines, I always check to see if the person who wrote it has ever been a paying customer of mine; the answer is always no. The bottom line is that I'm happy that my audience, in effect, vets itself. That way I can focus more time and energy on my paying and vetted potential customers.

These days consumers buy and make choices often based on alignment with their own values. By not focusing on infinite growth or assuming that more is better, a company of one can focus on making its products better align with the values of a smaller, more specific group of people, and then market directly to their needs and viewpoints. That way, if others outside that group hate what you do or what you stand for, it doesn't matter — you're not going after them as customers in the first place. Instead, you're drawing your own niche market closer by showing them your understanding and sympathy for how they see the world.

People can copy skills, expertise, and knowledge, which are all replicable with enough time and effort. What's not replicable is who you truly are — your style, your personality, your sense of activism, and your unique way of finding creative solutions to complicated problems. So lean on that in your work. Sell your *way of thinking* as much as you would a commodity. Polarization can shorten a sales cycle because it forces customers into a quicker binary choice, to decided yes or no. After all, it's hard to make money from maybes.

To build and maintain your company of one, the sooner you learn how to distinguish your company's profile in a positive way, the sooner you will be able to find your precise audience and sustain your business. You need to be more aware of who you are and then strategically highlight the innate and unique aspects of your personality to ensure that your business keeps and holds the attention of your customers.

BEGIN TO THINK ABOUT:

- How you could infuse your own distinct and unique personality into your products and company image
- Where you could lean on what makes your business or product quirky or different to garner attention in the market

7

.

The One Customer

HERE ARE A HANDFUL OF restaurants I eat at where the staff remember my name and what I typically order. (They don't even need to bring me the menu.) The owner comes out at some point to chat a little, not to see if I want another drink or dessert, but just to catch up. Sometimes, when a new item is added to the menu, they'll bring over a plate of it, for free, looking for feedback. If my order is ever wrong, which is rare, they either provide more food or take something off the bill — without me saying anything other than that the order wasn't quite right.

With service like that, I eat at these places very regularly. If friends are in town, that's where we go. Sure, the food is great, but the fact that I'm treated well at these restaurants — like their most important customer — matters more in making me a regular and long-term patron.

It's a great feeling when an employee or business owner goes out of their way to be helpful. There's something quite memorable about a personal touch, or a business taking ownership of a problem and going out of its way to fix it.

This isn't a chapter on simply being a good business to the people who pay you because it's the right thing to do. There's overwhelming evidence that treating customers well, as if they're your one and only customer, drives value to your bottom line.

In short, helping your customers succeed and providing amazing service are good for business. A recent Harris Interactive survey showed that nine out of ten Americans were willing to spend more with companies that exhibited great customer service. The same survey showed that 79 percent of people bailed on a transaction or did not buy what they intended to because of a poor customer service experience. A study done by the White House Office of Consumer Affairs found that loyal customers, on average, were worth up to ten times as much as their first purchase. There's also the hidden cost of negative experiences — Ruby Newell-Legner, a twenty-five-year student of customer happiness, found that only 4 percent of customers actually voice their dissatisfaction to a business: a whopping 91 percent of dissatisfied customers simply don't ever return. And with online reviews and social media, bad customer service tends to be talked about much more than praise for good customer service — the internet loves to turn into a mob against companies that don't help or that wrong their customers.

With these stats in mind, it's puzzling that some growth-centric companies care more about new customer acquisition than retention or customer happiness. Just as Kate O'Neill found with her work for Magazines.com (Chapter 4), acquiring new customers costs far more than renewing customers (6 to 7 percent more, according to the White House study just cited). Making renewals is often a far more important metric to measure, but they won't happen unless your customers are loyal enough to want to renew.

The obsession of some companies with growth and acquisition — with chasing a supposedly ever-growing number of users — becomes something of a vanity metric to tout on their homepage or in investor slide decks. But the cost of rapid user acquisition is incredibly high — so much so that it usually results in less overall profit. Being a profit-focused company of one (fewer expenses increase revenue just as much as more profits do), you can forgo vapid user expansion at any price and concentrate instead on retaining, pleasing, and helping your customers. In the long run, this approach costs far less and aids your company far more.

A company of one has one massive asset when it comes to customer service: it can be delivered in a way that doesn't scale. A restaurant owner can remember my name and dinner order because she works the front of the house and has one location, with regular staff. Just like Charlie Bickford, who's the CEO of Excalibur Screwbolts but still regularly answers the phone at his small office. Or Basecamp's founders, who answer technical support requests. Relationships, when the company is smaller, can be built with regular and loyal customers, and those personal relationships can keep them loyal and happy.

As companies of one, we are very much in the people-serving business. It's critical that we listen to each of our customers and take full ownership in making sure they are pleased with our service level and then successful in their own lives. Customer service is a huge differentiating factor in why people choose the places where they want to spend their money. If you serve your customers well, they in turn become brand evangelists for your company: basically an unpaid sales force that reduces your need to hire more staff.

CDBaby, a service that lets independent musicians sell their music on platforms for iTunes, has a policy that, from 7:00 AM to 10:00 PM, every customer support call will be picked up by a real person within two rings. They have no voice mail or routing systems, and the phone can be answered by anyone from the CEO to the people in the warehouse. (Everyone is trained to help customers.) CDBaby focuses on treating its customers like friends, and friends don't route their personal phone number to an automated system that says, "Your call is important to us, please continue to hold." Similarly, the folks at Basecamp try to answer every support request within fifteen minutes — regardless of the time of day or night.

Good customer service isn't about simply achieving the norms of courtesy. Being prompt, answering questions, and treating customers with respect shouldn't be rewarded — such service should be expected. Where companies of one can thrive and stand out is in *exceeding those expectations*, through personal touches, building reciprocity, and treating customers like they're very important (hint: they are).

THE SECOND WAVE

Customer service over the last few years has gone through a bit of a renaissance. In the past, supporting and servicing customers were thought of as a cost, and in business it makes sense to cut costs as much as possible in order to increase profits. In this old way of thinking, automations were heavily leaned upon, from complex phone trees ("press 8, then 4, then 6, then 234, then the pound key to speak with an agent") to customer message boards and self-help automated services like online knowledge bases. The problem with this kind of approach was that, however much money it saved a company, it actually created unneeded barriers between the company and customers with a problem, forcing them to attempt to solve it themselves, often to their great frustration.

Today's second wave of customer service as practiced by some organizations — and it should be the customer service delivered by all companies of one — focuses on emotion and ease. A study from McKinsey showed that 70 percent of buying experiences are based more on how customers feel they are treated and less on the tangibles of a product. The feeling of being treated exceptionally well can only increase in the context of a second purchase or a subscription renewal, because the customer has already developed a feeling about how the first purchase went or how any support requests were handled.

This second wave of customer service bets that providing a

positive emotional experience for each customer will create more wins and higher profits. If you treat your customers like they're your one and only customer, they'll reciprocate that love for your brand by not only continuing to do business with you, but telling their own networks to do so as well. Instead of treating customer service like a cost or expense, you can view it as an investment in retention and acquisition, because you're essentially building a customer sales force through your support staff.

If customer happiness is the goal of customer service, your support center can become the main source of referrals. Referrals are a powerful way to gain new customers — research done by SmallBizTrends found that a staggering 83 percent of new business comes from word-of-mouth referrals. The best way to get customers talking about your business to people they know is to make sure they're happy with what you're doing for them and how you're providing help if they need it.

You don't get referrals by just meeting the standard expectations of customer service — people rarely find it worth mentioning to others that a company did just enough to help them but nothing more. You have to do much more than that to evangelize customers if you want them to talk about your company favorably. A great example is a now-infamous story from the tech world about a customer service call to RackSpace, an enterprise-level cloud hosting provider. The call center rep heard someone in the background of a support call mention that he was hungry and wonder about ordering something. She quietly put the customer on hold, ordered a pizza to be delivered to the address she had on file, and went back to assisting the customer with his problem. Twenty minutes later, still on the phone with the customer, she heard a knock in the background and told him to go answer the door, saying, "It's your pizza." The pleasant unexpected experience led to not only a very happy (and full) customer but also a story that would be shared thousands of times online. This is the kind of customer service that builds reciprocity: your customer gets something unexpected and then feels the need to help your business, not only by remaining loyal but also by telling others.

Referrals work because they build *trust by proxy*. A referral is credible because someone you trust is telling you that they trust a certain company or product. And since you trust the person telling you, that sense of trust is instant and immediate with the company or product as well.

Joel Klettke, an in-demand freelance writer, says that 80 to 90 percent of his good leads for potential clients come from word of mouth. When he's recommended by someone else, he's found that those leads come with healthy expectations for a project and the costs involved, as well as the assumption that he's an expert (not just a paid technician). Joel doesn't have to spend time or resources on sales pitches with these referrals, since they're already sold on working with him. He just has to determine whether the project is a good fit.

In my own service-based business, all of my leads came from word of mouth as well. Early on, I decided that instead of spending time and money on marketing and outbound sales campaigns, I'd invest those resources instead in making sure every client was absolutely happy about having decided to hire me. Happy clients then did sales pitches for me, unasked, by telling everyone they knew that I was the person to hire for design work. For over a decade (until I moved away from services into products), these word-of-mouth referrals created a waiting list a few months long.

Even product businesses like Trello — a SaaS (software as a service) that lets you collaborate on projects online — have grown their reach and customer numbers, mostly through word of mouth. Trello has had 100 percent organic growth (i.e., no paid ads) to more than ten million users simply because people talk about its product, often, and in places visible to large groups of people, like social media or blogs. Trello has even developed fun games (that loosely relate to their product, like "Taco Out") that help create shareable moments. With the core of their product being a free version, Trello can convert people who find out about it into customers with not much extra effort. Coupled with the ease of use and helpfulness of its software, Trello's massive (unpaid) sales force of customers tells everyone they know about this software.

LISTENING AND UNDERSTANDING: A LITTLE GOES A LONG WAY

Kate Leggett of Forrester Research found that keeping customers happy and helping them succeed reduce churn, increase the likelihood of repeat business, and even help in winning new business. In other words, when your customers win, you do too. In truth, your customers don't care if your business is profitable — but if you help them become profitable too, they'll never leave you.

Helping your customers as individuals requires as much empathy and care as it does to sell whatever it is you're offering them. You have to be able to understand your customers and their needs to serve them effectively.

Lady Geek, a London-based consultancy, developed an "empathy index" (published in the *Harvard Business Review*) that combines publicly available information and proprietary data to rank global companies based on how empathetic they are — toward both their customers and their own employees. The five most profitable companies on the index rank at the top of the empathy scale. For example, number-three LinkedIn (with an empathy score of 98.82) is not afraid to go where its users are, even if that's a rival platform like Twitter, which ranks twenty-fourth (with an empathy score of 86.47). This approach illustrates that LinkedIn puts the needs, interests, and choices of its customers above its own business objectives — which pays off by increasing LinkedIn's bottom line.

The more you understand your customers — their needs, wants, motivations, and desires — the more you can feel with them and the better you can serve them. This kind of customer service is more than just the lip-service corporate speak of "you matter to us." This is customer service that takes specific actions and puts strategies into place that begin with listening and move toward understanding.

There's a common misconception that empathy is for weak, nonprofit, hippie-lifestyle businesses, but in fact it's a most useful tool to drive real profit. This comes down to several simple facts: the more you understand your customers, the more you can tailor and position products that provide real value to them, the more you can help them with support requests, and the more you can learn from them, because customers understand buyers better than you do. After all, they are buyers.

The first step in treating customers empathetically is listening to their needs; with this knowledge, we can drive innovations or new product ideas. MIT's Eric von Hippel has produced a substantial body of research showing that a resounding number of profitable innovations within companies have originated with customers — more than 60 percent. With this research in hand, 3M's Medical-Surgical Markets Division tried to fix its poor innovation record in the 1990s by creating some new products based on information from "lead users." Within five years, the results were quite dramatic: the division was bringing in $146 million in average revenue from user-lead innovations, compared to $18 million in average revenue from internally led innovations.

Understanding customers requires not just providing exceptional handling of their support requests but then gaining a bigger-picture idea about the types of questions and requests that are coming in. Even in a company of one, it's important to recognize the general theme of each request and to manage it in a way that makes patterns and clues in the data discernible later on. It helps to see patterns by organizing all feedback and suggestions in a central location. For example, if you find that support requests are primarily on a certain topic, maybe you could do a better job of teaching users about that topic. And if a handful of requests on a certain topic continue to come up again and again, perhaps that topic can be the basis of your next user-led innovation initiative.

Best Buy is a stellar example of a company that doesn't just listen to customers but actually takes time to understand customer feedback and put it to use. The company shares customer reviews on its website with vendors to encourage them to improve their products based on what customers want. Best Buy also rewards many customers who provide feedback by giving them incentives and discounts on store purchases.

Sometimes empathy in larger companies takes the form of refusing to let bureaucratic red tape get in the way of helping a customer. A few years ago, an elderly man was snowed in and stranded in his rural Pennsylvania home during the holidays. When his out-of-town daughter found out, she began calling grocery stores in his area to see if any would deliver food to him, since he didn't have enough to weather the storm. After calling several stores — none of which offered home delivery as a service — she called Trader Joe's. The employee said that it was not Trader Joe's policy to deliver, nor was it a service they typically provided, but given the extreme circumstances they'd gladly get food delivered to her father. After she provided a list, the employee even suggested additional items that would fit her father's low-sodium diet. When it came time to arrange payment for the order, the employee said not to worry about it — the order and delivery would be free of charge — and to have a happy holiday. Thirty minutes later, the order was at her father's house, having cost nothing. Empathy in business can sometimes mean just being a caring human being.

Like the pizza delivery story, this story captivates us because it reminds us that some companies are less interested in "business as usual" and their bottom line than in keeping customers happy and taking care of them as fellow human beings. Even though most companies say that customers are their top priority, it's uncommonly rare to see that idea put into practice. But in going far beyond the extra mile, this kind of extraordinary service turns customers into loyal and raving fans. These are the kinds of stories that get shared, and being talked about far and wide can only benefit a business.

In short, customer happiness is the new marketing. If your customers feel that you are taking care of them, then they'll stick around and they'll tell others. This is the precise way in which companies of one can compete with behemoths in their market — by outsupporting them. It's much harder to compete with bigger companies on aspects like volume, low prices, or logistics. But it's much easier as a smaller business to compete on the personal touches — going the extra mile and treating customers like humans, not numbers. That's a major advantage for any company of one.

SUCCESSFUL CUSTOMERS BUILD SUCCESSFUL BUSINESSES

Since financial success (i.e., profit) ensures longevity, most business owners naturally spend a great deal of time thinking about how they can make their businesses more successful. But what most business owners or even team leaders often fail to consider is their customers' success. After all, your successful customer has the financial means to continue to support your business, which in turn increases your profit. So your customers' success leads to your business succeeding as well.

When a company looks at customers as impersonal transactions or orders, it's easy for that relationship to devolve into one focused on how much money can be made from them with the least amount of money spent. But a company that believes customers represent relationships that can be both mutually beneficial and long-term succeeds when its customers succeed.

Adam Waid, the director of the Customer Success Department at SalesForce Pardot, doesn't want to take chances with helping customers find wins. In fact, Customer Success — devoted to providing training, implementation assistance, best-practice recommendations, and ongoing support — is the company's largest department. This effort has made SalesForce Pardot the number-one most innovative company according to *Forbes* magazine, and its customers have seen an average 34 percent increase in sales revenue through the help offered by its Customer Success Department.

Cindy Carson, the director of Customer Success at UserIQ, believes that the most successful customers are those who start off on the right footing, with tailored onboarding processes. Her team even looks at each customer's user case for their software to fully understand how UserIQ can benefit them the most; then they provide segmented training that highlights the specifics that will help each customer gain wins.

Growth often happens organically in a customer-first approach, based on realized profits, because even though you're entirely focusing on customers' success, the by-product is growth in your customer base from their slow and steady evolution into your sales force.

Jeff Sheldon, who runs Ugmonk, a boutique clothing line for designers, is obsessed with quality — in both the products he creates and sells and the support his customers receive. If a shirt doesn't fit quite right or something is wrong with an order, he'll ship a new shirt right away and not even require that the wrong order be sent back. Because Ugmonk takes care of them, customers take care of Ugmonk by routinely posting links to the company on social media, with photos of them wearing Ugmonk clothes. Sheldon receives a lot of free publicity from industry influencers and magazines talking about Ugmonk and his obsession with the quality of his products.

Focusing on customer success is a mentality and a way of doing business for a company of one that encompasses all aspects of a business. It begins before a product is even created, with planning to make sure everything is done correctly and is of the best quality. This way of doing business includes customer education (which we'll talk about in Chapter 9) to improve their skill set and foster their success.

Some companies view some customers as too small to matter, especially when it comes to success. But if you take this shortsighted view, you may wrongly assume that your customer's situation or size won't ever change. After all, your own company of one, with its focus on being better rather than bigger, might also be thought of as "too small to matter" by the companies where you're a customer. In adopting this kind of mind-set, you lose sight of your own customers' long-term strategic importance and loyalty. A customer who pays $10 a month for a service and sticks around for ten years is worth a lot more than a customer who pays $100 a month but cancels your service after only a few months. Smaller businesses can also wield a lot of influence, since they can easily amass large followings on social media and massive mailing lists (both of which can scale your company with no need to grow).

Finally, to be the most helpful to your customers, you sometimes have to look beyond the problems they're presenting to you. The underlying reason customers are asking for help is often not obvious: sometimes they're looking for specific answers, but sometimes they're asking for a certain feature without even being aware that's what they're doing. For example, when I was doing web design, clients would often want me to design a site that, in their words, would simply look great. Over time, though, I realized that wasn't the main reason most customers wanted to hire me: what they really wanted was a site that would look great but also generate more revenue. When I changed my sales pitch and began speaking about how good design could help a potential customer achieve more profit, the number of projects I landed from sales calls more than doubled.

Listening to what your customers really need and want is key for companies of one.

WHEN THINGS GO WRONG (AND THINGS ARE GOING TO GO WRONG)

It's not a matter of if, it's a matter of when. Every business has so many moving parts, so many places to interact with customers, and is typically so reliant on at least a few suppliers or partners that mistakes can and will sometimes happen. Trying to avoid mistakes at all costs, or pretending that mistakes never happen, is not a viable strategy. More realistic is having a plan for when they do happen.

Just as the transparency discussed in Chapter 3 is important internally for both leaders and employees, it's equally important to be transparent outwardly with your customers. That doesn't mean sharing everything, but it does mean being open about your company's relevant highs and lows, as they could have an effect on your customer relationship. If your business has been treating customers empathetically, they'll tend to be more understanding when things go wrong—but only if you immediately work to fix or resolve issues.

You have to *own your mistakes*—even those caused by someone else—by taking personal responsibility for them before someone else blames you for them. The first step is apologizing like a real, empathetic human, not a corporate PR-sounding robot. Customers don't expect perfect — they just expect problems to be dealt with fairly, empathetically, and quickly.

A few years ago, the vendor I used to collect payment from my customers had a software bug that double-charged dozens of people. They ended up paying $600 for a $300 product, which none of them were happy about (to say the least). It felt like the worst-case scenario: I was taking more money from my customers than they had agreed to pay for my product.

Although technically it was the software vendor's fault, since it was their software that had a bug in it, I took full responsibility — because it was my company's name on the store that sold the product. I immediately emailed every single person affected — even those who didn't yet realize they'd been double-charged — and informed them of the steps I was taking to prevent the mistake from happening again (switching vendors, at great cost to my company in time and money) and my plan to return their money as quickly as possible. I ended the email with my phone number in case they had questions or concerns. Of the dozens of customers affected, only two asked for full refunds (the $300 double-charge refund plus the original $300 cost of the product).

Although I definitely had a couple of irate customers — and I couldn't blame them for that — most people were understanding and acknowledged that software can involve bugs. And by taking a hit to my bottom line and absorbing the costs of switching vendors, I helped secure my customers' confidence that I was working toward making things right. What I learned from this experience was the importance of treating my customers the way I'd want to be treated if the situation had been reversed. I couldn't have done that by either "ostriching" (sticking my head in the sand and hoping not many customers would notice the blip of a double-charge followed by a refund) or saving money by continuing with the bug-filled vendor software. The long-term strategy of keeping loyal customers who were happy with my product trumped the short-term cash loss.

Some companies don't allow employees to apologize in any way because they fear the legal consequences of admitting fault. Unfortunately, this approach can make customers angry, especially if all they want is to hear someone owning a mistake. This book is definitely not offering legal advice, but it's worth noting here the 2015 *New York Times* report that doctors who are transparent about errors and offer apologies to patients are actually sued far less for malpractice than doctors who deny wrongdoing and defend mistakes. Two years after the University of Illinois adopted this practice of transparency, with full apologies, its malpractice filings dropped by half. A separate study by Nottingham University found that in most cases apologizing costs nothing—companies that simply apologize for mistakes and work to fix them fare better even than companies that offer financial compensation.

Acknowledgment of fault is powerful. It shows empathy, a willingness to own the problem, and a desire to then fix it. And as the studies cited here all found, apologizing effectively can cost dramatically less than a lawsuit or a refund. But an apology doesn't work if you're not genuinely sorry—most people can sense a disingenuous corporate "sorry." Before you respond, give yourself time to understand the situation and fully listen to the complaint. This usually involves validating a customer's wronged feelings, being transparent about what happened, and clearly detailing how you'll fix the problem and ensure that it doesn't happen again.

Companies of one need to turn complaints into opportunities to do better and use them to attempt to build closer relationships with the customers who stick around. A company that doesn't both listen to and understand complaints does so at its peril. For example, in 2011 Netflix ignored its customers' requests and split apart its DVD and streaming businesses, effectively increasing its prices by 40 percent. As a result of that strictly cost-saving move (and not listening to their customers), Netflix stock fell to half its previous value, the company lost 800,000 customers, and it was soon ranked as one of the ten most-hated companies in America, based on a survey done by 24/7WallSt.

These days, of course, most consumers take to social media to complain about mistakes or missteps by companies. A study done by Liel Leibovitz, a communications professor at New York University, found that 88 percent of consumers were less likely to buy from a company that didn't answer support requests on social media. And for customers who took to social media to voice their concerns about a product they had purchased, 45 percent said that they'd be mad if they received no response and 27 percent said that they would completely stop doing business with that company. We have to pay attention to our customers in the places where they're spending their time — on Facebook and Twitter.

YOUR WORD IS A CONTRACT

Nicholas Epley, a professor of behavioral science at the University of Chicago Business School, says that maintaining good business relationships with customers doesn't require superhuman efforts. Rather, you simply need to do what you say you'll do and customers will be grateful.

Nicholas says that people tend to evaluate each other based on two general dimensions: how interpersonally warm we appear to be, and how competent we seem to be. His work suggests that the way to be positively assessed by others is by making promises, and then keeping them. This advice is especially important to companies that serve customers, since customers who are treated with warmth, understanding, and competence turn into loyal customers.

As a company of one, you have to be very careful in what you tell your customers, or even potential customers, because your word is your social contract with them. It doesn't do you any good to overpromise the effectiveness of your products or pitch false information, even unintentionally. In these days when almost all information is available online, you need to be clear about what your business does and how you do it. Is your data secure? Are your overseas factories safe and paying fair wages? Did your car rank well on Insurance Institute for Highway Safety crash tests? Are the companies in your socially responsible exchange-traded funds lobbying against environmental concerns?

Several studies, like one done by Luigi Zingales of the University of Chicago, have shown that businesses with a culture of keeping their word are much more profitable than those that go back on their word or only say things that don't align with their actions. He finds that proclaimed values are completely irrelevant without proof that those values are backed by corporate actions.

What does it take for a company to keep its promise? And why do so many businesses fail to keep their promises? This "commitment drift," as Maryam Kouchaki, Elizabeth Doty, and Francesca Gino describe it, is defined as systematic breakdowns in fulfilling a company's most important commitments to its stakeholders. These researchers believe that commitment drift stems from several factors that are related to a business's perceived short-term gains and that end up compromising the stated promise. To avoid going back on a promise, a business needs to put a few strategies into practice, from leadership to customer service reps.

The first strategy is to make fewer and better commitments

to customers. A business that believes it should "underpromise and overdeliver" sometimes fails to even simply deliver on par with expectations. Next, a company that isn't tracking its commitments — for example, through support system software or by noting promises from leadership — can easily forget what the original promise was. Finally, having actual processes in place to meet these commitments is required; assuming that such processes won't be relevant until sometime in the future will only lead to broken promises. By focusing on these three strategies, companies can learn how to better keep promises to their customers.

The best approach is to treat every agreement with a customer (or even an employee) as a legally binding contract because, on a societal level, that's what it is. If you promise to give someone something at a certain time, then do it, and do it on time. Whether it's a quote or a deliverable or a customer service response doesn't matter. If you aren't sure whether you can deliver, either say that you can't deliver or negotiate for a longer delivery time so that you can be sure you will.

Anytime you don't keep your word you're not just letting down one person or one business — you're losing the opportunity to work with every single contact of that person or business, because you can be sure that they won't ever send business your way. Or worse, they'll tell everyone they know that you don't keep your word. A broken promise balloons outward, like our ever-expanding universe: you ruin not just your relationship with one potential client or contact but your chance to work with everyone else they know.

Bear all that in mind the next time a problem pops up in your day-to-day business. If you want your company of one to succeed, it's essential to do the right thing when it comes to owning mistakes and errors.

BEGIN TO THINK ABOUT:

- What you could do to ensure that your existing customers feel both happy and acknowledged
- Where you could exceed expectations with your customer service
- How you could create opportunities for word of mouth and referrals
- How you own and then fix mistakes
- What you could do to ensure that your customers end up with wins

8

.

Scalable Systems

I F THE POINT OF A company of one is to question growth and challenge scale, the answer might sometimes be that growth is in fact required — when it aligns with your overall purpose. When growth in profit, customers, or reach is needed, however, companies of one can look to simple and repeatable systems to facilitate scale, with no need for more employees or resources.

Marshall Haas, cofounder of Need/Want, used to think that a company needs to scale in proportion to the revenue it generates. Thus, a $100 million business needs to have at least hundreds of employees and several layers of bureaucratic managerial hierarchy. What he's found in practice, though, is that, with fewer than ten employees, his company can grow very slowly and still increase revenue — which is currently at nearly $10 million.

Most people would assume that only tech startups or software companies could manage to scale revenue far quicker than they add employees and expenses, since their products exist in the ether of the web. But Need/Want, a physical product company that sells everything from bedding to notebooks to iPhone cases, has managed to build a big business with only a tiny team.

Need/Want uses scalable systems and channels to increase profits. They use prepackaged software, Shopify, to run their online store, which can handle anywhere from one order a day to over a million. They stay out of big-box stores, so they don't need a dedicated outside sales team. They don't do trade shows, and all their marketing efforts stem from a team of three who focus entirely on online channels, like social media, paid ads, and a newsletter (all of which can increase reach without too many extra resources to manage).

Need/Want outsources manufacturing to a factory with which they have a close relationship; it can handle anything from handfuls of orders to tens of thousands of orders in a day. The company also outsources shipping and fulfillment to a trusted partner. In other words, Need/Want is a perfect example of a company of one that utilizes scalable systems. Its direct-to-consumer sales model keeps things lean and enables the company to really experiment with the best way to find and sell to new consumers.

The company started when founders Marshall Haas and Jon Wheatley became interested in applying the knowledge they'd acquired from working at tech firms to physical products. Prior to their partnership, Marshall was making money selling products that you couldn't actually touch (software), and Jon was creating things that could be touched, but without making any real money (VC-based startups that never got off the ground or made any profits).

They treat their company like a tech startup, but instead of selling software, they sell products, relying heavily on technology, automations, and the scalability of online channels. Their team, even at nearly $10 million in yearly revenue, remains small: besides Marshall and Jon, who run the business and handle marketing, there's a head of operations, four support staff (two of whom are part-time), a CFO, and a developer. When they require more help, they hire freelancers and contractors and outsource until it's cheaper to bring the job in-house. That is, they hire only when it's too painful or time-consuming not to, or when the salary for a hire could easily be justified by the return on investment. The Need/Want model is growth based on *realized* profit, not growth based on *potential* profit (the model adopted by most startups or VC-backed companies). They operate out of St. Louis, where it's far cheaper to rent office space and to live, rather than in a typical startup hub like San Francisco or New York.

Because Need/Want's heavy reliance on social media and newsletters, which are both infinitely scalable systems, creates a one-to-many relationship, the company doesn't need more staff to reach more people. They simply need increasingly effective messaging and positioning—which they're always testing with tools like A/B tests in their ad campaigns and email campaigns. A/B tests let a company test a few variations of a small subset of a list, see which variant performs best, and then send the winning variant to the rest of the list.

James Clear—the author and photographer introduced in Chapter 2—has developed scalable systems in his own business, which creates and promotes digital products. With a mailing list that has more than 400,000 subscribers and increases by 1,000 new people per week, he could have his pick of goods to create and sell to them. His focus for paid offerings follows two simple rules that help him remain a company of one (with a single assistant) and serve both the many people in his audience and the people who buy his products.

James's first rule is that his products must take little to no management. The digital courses he sells have no ongoing live webinars or training sessions—customers merely buy the content and then watch the prerecorded videos in their own time. His second rule is to charge a onetime fee for everything he offers; he accepts no retainers and no ongoing consulting work. To give a keynote speech, he'll fly in, give the talk, answer questions, and then be gone the next morning. These two rules help James keep his business small, his overhead and expenses light, and,

most of all, his time freed up to do what he wants to do: researching, writing, and sharing. By creating goods and offering services
that are scalable without any actual major scaling on his part, he's
optimized his profitable business for the life he wants.

Of course, most people and businesses don't work backwards
like James did. People tend to start with a business model and
then become unhappy when their days are filled with tasks they
don't enjoy. Instead of thinking, *What product can I create?* or
What service can I offer, James believes that we should first think:
What type of life do I want? and *How do I want to spend my days?*
Then you can work backwards from there into a business model
that allows you to create scalable systems to deliver your product
to your audience.

Let's break all of this down further by looking at how systems
can be put into place to assist companies of one with creation,
connection, collaboration, and support.

CREATION AS A SCALABLE SYSTEM

It's not news that companies separate product ideas, marketing,
and sales from physical production. If done poorly, this practice
can create problems ranging from low ethical standards and unfair wages to vast amounts of waste as a side effect of manufacturing.

In the beginning of separating branding from production,
large companies believed that great fortunes could be made by
achieving the lowest common denominator in production, and in
recent years that belief has been propelled by the forces of globalization. According to author and activist Naomi Klein, however,
globalization has had negative effects on workers, including poor
conditions, low salaries, and unfair treatment. Klein believes
that a new movement, one very much in line with the mind-set
of companies of one, is breaking away from global brands with

questionable morals that focus on maximizing profits over people, and that this movement will shift businesses toward slower, smaller, or on-demand strategies, making them more "fair" in all senses of the word.

For example, trend-setting companies like Arthur & Henry advocate for "slow fashion" and encourage customers to wear their clothing longer, and in stages — first at the office when a garment is fresh and new; then casually on the weekend, rolling up frayed sleeves; and then, when stains and small tears appear, for garden work. Ideally, the final stage for a worn-out Arthur & Henry garment is use as a rag in the garage. When we extract every ounce of usefulness from each piece of clothing by reusing it over and over, we get the most out of the work of the farmer, the miller, the tailor, and the factory employee. Arthur & Henry's metric for success is sustainability in all forms: earning steady revenues, raising money for charities, minimizing environmental damage, and maximizing benefits to all workers.

Another example of a beneficial separation between brand and factory that has resulted in an ethical and profitable scalable system for a company of one is Girlfriend Collective, founded by Ellie Dinh and Quang Dinh. They sell bras and leggings that are manufactured in Taiwan, using mostly recycled plastic from used water bottles. Girlfriend Collective advocates for slow fashion and against pumping out large numbers of poorly made products; although its product order wait times can sometimes be long as a result, customers are happy to wait. The company pays workers 125 percent higher than minimum wage and offers free catered lunches, guided exercise breaks, health insurance, and free health checkups every six months. Its environmental practices exceed government standards for manufacturing as well as for recycling and waste water management.

Many overseas factories turn out vast numbers of brand-company products, which helps them stay busy and keep costs low:

when one partner company sends in a smaller order, a factory can switch to producing for another company with a larger order. Not tied to any one brand, an overseas factory can work with any number of partner companies. This practice sometimes slows down production, but it also creates a more sustainable, almost-on-demand system in which production never outweighs demand.

CONNECTION AS A SCALABLE SYSTEM

By constantly working toward reducing one-to-one points of contact with customers and focusing instead on one-to-many relationships, a company of one can scale its connection with customers without actually scaling its business. Yes, personal touches, as we saw in Chapter 7, are essential, and direct communication with customers is always required to learn, empathize, adapt, and revise — yet the majority of connecting can be done en masse.

A perfect example is email marketing. It requires the same amount of effort to send an email to 50,000 people as it does to send that same email to one person. This is precisely why most companies of one rely heavily on newsletters and email automation: these are powerful tools for building relationships, trust, and even revenue. With an average return on investment of 3,800 percent, according to the Data & Marketing Association, email marketing is a valid model for scaling without scale.

Systems for connections don't work simply by turning them on and watching them increase profits. (This would be like believing you can plant a real money tree.) Work is required, at the outset and through iteration, to ensure that these systems are functioning optimally. And as discussed in Chapter 6, personality is still required, even with automated customer communication, in order for these systems to be effective. The point of scalable connecting is to make customers and potential customers feel as though they're getting on-demand information as they need it, not being relegated to an infinite loop of unhelpful and frustrating computer-generated responses.

Using personalization and segmentation in connection channels like email is key. You want to send the right email, to the right person, at the right time. Otherwise, you may be sending out a firehose blast of messages that may not even be relevant — like a sales pitch to a customer who's already purchased the product. Tools like MailChimp are great for filtering and targeting an audience, allowing you to send emails with product pitches only to people who have not yet purchased the product, or notices of in-store sales only to people who live in the particular geographic location, or up/cross sells only to people who already own the relevant products. Also, a study done by Campaign Monitor showed that emails with personalized subject lines are 26 percent more likely to be opened. The Epsilon Email Institute found that segmented automation emails have a 70.5 percent higher open rate and a 152 percent higher click-through rate than "business as usual" firehose blasts.

To increase the effectiveness and the conversion rates of connection channels, you need to do careful testing. Luckily, systems like email marketing software allow for A/B tests. Similar A/B tests can also be run with marketing messaging on websites to increase engagement and commerce.

In my own business, email marketing accounts for more than 93 percent of revenue each year. It allows me to connect with thousands of people who have opted to receive updates, education information in the form of articles, and even product pitches. I can write a single email that is instantly delivered to 30,000 people. I can teach 10,000 paying customers how to use my products without communicating with each of them every day.

Newsletter automation can also be used to increase customer education and retention at scale. Automated emails sent to people immediately after purchase can show these customers how to best use the product they purchased or answer common customer questions, greatly reducing customer support requests. Automated updates and notes and even simple check-ins with customers after a set amount of time can also increase the likelihood that customers will keep using the product, as well as the likelihood that they'll tell others about their purchase (for instance, via social media sharing buttons within the emails).

Even companies of one that focus on client services, such as consultants or freelancers, can use automation software to reduce the amount of one-to-one contact during interactions, whether it's onboarding new customers or following up after a project is finished.

Jamie Leigh Hoogendoorn, a designer and student in my "Creative Class" course, vastly cut down the amount of time she was spending dealing with emails from "tire-kickers." By automating most of her onboarding process with automated emails that delivered information about her services and prices and setting up a calendar system that let people pick a date and time to speak to her (based on her own calendar's availability), she cut down the amount of time it took her to take a lead and turn it into a paying project from between eight to sixteen hours to only one hour. Her success rate for winning bids has increased, since her potential clients get information on her services instantly, instead of having to wait for her to reply to their emails. And Jamie's warm and stylish personality still shines through in all of the automations she uses.

SaaS is becoming more prevalent, and so too are the tools that allow us to spend less time on the minutiae of operating a company of one and more time on our core work, all while helping us scale our reach or profit with no need to also scale our time, staff, or expenses.

COLLABORATION AS
A SCALABLE SYSTEM

Working *for* yourself doesn't necessarily mean working *by* yourself. Even if your company of one is just you, there are still times when you'll need to collaborate with others — from contractors to partners to clients. If your company of one is a small team or exists within an organization, even more layers of collaboration are required. But collaboration is a double-edged sword: technology allows us to easily connect with each other in real time, but at the expense of focused, deep work.

In the past, internal communication had to be face-to-face, in meetings or on scheduled conference calls, but as workplaces move toward remote workers and flex hours such communication is becoming less and less efficient. Increasingly common corporate messaging tools, like Slack, intranets, and cheap or free VOIP calling, are allowing groups located all over the world to not just work together but truly collaborate.

With these collaboration tools, however, many companies may unknowingly be filling their employees' time with always-on distractions, especially if employees are required to keep their status as "available," share their calendars, and keep up with group messaging all day. Real-time messaging can turn into all-day meetings, every single day, with no set agenda.

Samuel Hulick, founder of User Onboarding, believes that tools like Slack are "asyncronish": they're neither truly real-time (you sometimes have to wait indefinitely for an answer) or asynchronous (meaning no immediate response is expected). While the use of messaging tools can seem like a truly great advance in collaboration, too often they lead to daylong half-conversations, like a slow-drip coffee maker.

Real-time collaboration can be very useful when a whole team is required to brainstorm or solve a problem together, but it can also be completely distracting if it's expected most of the time. This is why companies like Basecamp and Buffer tell employees to disconnect from the distractions of collaboration for most of their day. No one at these companies, for example, is expected to be immediately available, unless there is an emergency (which is quite rare). In general, responses are expected at these companies within days, not minutes.

By allowing collaboration to grow from face-to-face contact to notifications on all our digital devices, even the ones we use outside of work (like phones and tablets), we've let it scale beyond what makes for focused and efficient work.

Scaled collaboration does make sense when a project can't be advanced without input from several team members. A perfect example is what is known as a "hackathon" — a combination of the words "hack" (exploratory programming, not computer crimes) and "marathon." In a hackathon, several small teams of developers, designers, and project managers are formed, each group collaborating, with speed and focus, to complete a large project over the course of several hours or a few days. Their work has a specific focus — for example, coming up with a new feature for a piece of a software that a company sells, or designing a new website, as the City of New York did, for local government to use in building relationships with the private sector. At the end of a hackathon, each team presents a series of demonstrations to share its results with the rest of the group.

Hugely successful innovations have come out of hackathons — for example, Facebook's "Like" button. Hackathons work because they are focused collaboration, not 24/7 "be available at all times" collaboration. They can be fun, energetic, and highly productive, since everyone is collaborating on a common goal and purpose. And once the hackathon is over, everyone goes back to their regular jobs.

Elsewhere in this chapter, I advise scaling up certain aspects of your business, but collaboration is the one area where companies of one should *scale down* — from an environment of always-on, always-available, slow-drip messaging distractions to a regimen of clearly defined times to work together to accomplish large tasks together. Otherwise, you run the risk of being available for distraction during every hour of every day.

BEGIN TO THINK ABOUT:

- Where you could use automation and technology to scale so your business doesn't have to
- How you could outsource tasks that require massive scale
- How you could add personalization and segmentation to your one-to-many communication channels

9

■

Teach Everything You Know

BRIAN CLARK STARTED OUT IN the mid-1990s as a practicing attorney, with a great job at a reputable law firm. The only problem was that he wanted to be a writer — and not just any writer, but a writer with full control over what he wrote and how his writing was published. And he wanted to use this new medium called the internet to do it.

So he quit his law job and began writing about pop culture, attempting to make money by selling ads and affiliated offers through his website. Unfortunately, these revenue streams didn't bring in enough money to pay the bills. So Brian began to learn about marketing, mostly through the work of marketing guru Seth Godin, who was writing about building mailing list audiences and selling your own products instead of ads for other people's products.

Brian took the next step. Since he still had his law degree and was running out of funds, Brian started a website that combined his love of writing with his experience practicing law. In law school, he had been taught that young lawyers need to get jobs at established firms because it's the more senior lawyers in these firms who have the clients. Having decided that he wanted to find his own clients instead, Brian decided to do so by teaching people who wanted to learn from lawyers about legal issues. Freely

sharing information with them on a weekly basis proved fruit-
ful: because he was writing educational content, people trusted
his expertise and then wanted to hire, not just any lawyer, but
the person who was sharing the information they needed. Brian
quickly built up a huge roster of people eager to hire him to solve
their own legal issues.

However, Brian still didn't want to practice law. Taking an in-
terim step toward the business he now runs, he decided to focus on an industry that had both the money to pay well and a
low starting point of knowledge about the internet: real estate. He
took what he had learned about internet content marketing and
sharing information with an audience and founded two very focused real estate brokerages. Within a year, he was making more
money than he would have if he had become a partner in the first
law firm he worked at.

The problem was that, amid this great success, Brian was
burned out. Although he was excellent at marketing and online
education, he was a terrible manager for his growing companies.
His two brokerages required a lot of work because, having never
documented the processes involved in running them, he ended
up just doing most of the work himself. Then, in 2005, he had a
catastrophic snowboarding accident that left him unable to work
for several months. He used his convalescence as an opportunity
to sell both brokerages, but since neither of the new owners knew
what was involved in running them (and Brian's lack of docu-
mentation certainly didn't help), they both went under soon after.

Brian started CopyBlogger as a side business at first. He hadn't
saved enough money prior to his accident to go full-time with it,
so he was doing a lot of consulting work just to pay the bills. But
the internet was starting to notice how content, sharing, and education could come together as a legitimate form of marketing for
any business. And so CopyBlogger, a business focused on teach-

ing companies how to use content marketing, gradually began to thrive.

With his previous online real estate businesses, Brian learned that his competitive edge was in his ability to outshare his competition, and that's what he did with CopyBlogger—he shared everything he knew about content marketing with a quickly growing audience. Brian believes that building an audience by sharing content with a growing mailing list is a solid business model, in that you can find out exactly what your growing audience wants from you and then build it for them. He learned from Seth Godin that selling to people who truly want to hear from you, because you've been sharing with them, is far more effective than interrupting strangers online who don't even know you. Each year this idea was proven correct, as every product CopyBlogger launched was more and more successful. Each product was based on direct intel from interacting with and listening to the audience consuming the content that Brian was sharing. This "education through content" built the necessary trust to turn into sales.

Of course, the stereotypical model for selling is manipulation: pressuring potential customers until they give in and buy, like the proverbial pushy used-car salesperson. But great salespeople—from car dealers to real estate agents to B2B sellers—know sales increase when you honestly evaluate what someone needs and then teach them the value of what you're selling. (If your product doesn't fit their needs, you need to let them know that as well.) Sharing content and information is an effective way to begin a sales process because it helps a potential customer see what they need, why they need it, and then how your products can help solve their problem.

CopyBlogger, now renamed RainMaker Digital, has capitalized on this "share everything" mentality: it now does more than $12 million in annual revenue and has more than 200,000 customers buying content management software, online courses, and Word-Press themes. The company's success has flowed not from a commitment to achieving higher profits or more sales, but from focusing entirely on what its audience needs to learn and then teaching them that (through free articles and paid digital products). And obviously, the company has been rewarded for correct prioritization.

To stand out and build an audience as a company of one, you have to out-teach and outshare the competition, not outscale them. This approach has several positive outcomes.

The first is that creating a relationship with an audience that sees you as a teacher sets you up to be perceived as the domain expert on the subject matter. If you're teaching an audience about legal issues on the internet each week in a newsletter, they'll begin to trust your insights, and then, as happened with Brian, you'll probably be the first person they think of when they need to hire someone to help them with legal issues.

The second benefit of out-teaching your competition is the chance to show an audience the benefits of what you're selling. For example, if you're selling a plug-in electric vehicle, teaching people the benefits of this type of vehicle — how much they'll save by not buying gas each year, why and how it's safer than a gas vehicle, the vehicle's reduced environmental impact, and so on — shows them all the reasons they'd want to buy from you, without overtly selling to them. You're simply giving them the information they need, in a genuine, compelling, and educational way, and letting them come to their own decision about whether such a purchase is right for them.

The third reason teaching works is that by educating new customers on how best to use your product or service and showing them how to get the most out of it or how to be the most successful with it, you also ensure that they'll become long-term customers and tell others about their positive experience.

The final reason teaching works for a company of one is that, except for certain proprietary information—like your unexecuted ideas, business strategies, or patentable technologies—most ideas or processes don't need to be kept under lock and key. Being transparent in almost all areas, while running your company aboveboard, can only help build trust with your customers.

IDEAS ALONE ARE WORTHLESS

How many people have you heard say something along the lines of "I had the idea for [Amazon, Zappos, Google] long before it existed—I should be rich!" But ideas aren't a valid currency. Execution is the only valid currency in business.

To clarify, as this can feel like a fairly controversial point to make, an idea alone is worthless because it stands *outside* of execution. So, for example, the idea itself, that growth should be questioned, is something I've been sharing for years online, in my newsletter and podcasts and with anyone who'll listen. Sharing the idea in a copyrighted book, however, is different. The purpose of the copyright is not to protect the idea (it'd be great if more people wrote about this subject, and I encourage that), but to protect the execution—the months of research and writing that went into formulating the specific words and flow of this book. Protecting intellectual property is important, but protecting general ideas is not, because if all you have is an idea, you've not done the work yet.

Sharing your ideas far and wide helps build not just a following for what you're selling but a movement around the core values and thinking that your product stands for. Having even more books, research, and ideas flowing around the idea of questioning growth ultimately helps both this book and others like it.

The idea for UFC—a mixed martial arts organization—started in 1993, but those attempting to make it a reality almost went bankrupt, owing to rules and government opposition. In other words, the idea was there but the execution was not — so it was unprofitable. It wasn't until two casino moguls became involved and had rule changes implemented that complied with government standards that UFC turned into a $1 billion business. The idea wasn't enough on its own to make the UFC business thrive; it needed the right execution (and the right people involved to manage the execution).

At the core of many massive, profitable, global companies is an old idea executed exceptionally well. Facebook is just a better MySpace, and both are essentially digital meeting places. Taxis take people from point A to point B. Uber/Lyft just figured out how to make this service more convenient. None of these are billion-dollar ideas; rather, they're billion-dollar executions of ideas. That's why companies of one shouldn't worry about sharing their ideas, as long as they're taking care of execution and their ideas are not proprietary.

There are also very few completely new ideas. Most ideas just riff off existing companies, plans, ideas, or solutions. By focusing a lot of time and energy on protecting ideas instead of sharing them, you run the risk of not letting them get better through critical feedback from others. Even sharing your business idea with potential customers has its benefits, as they can weigh in early, before you've invested a lot of time or resources, and help you shape and position the idea into an even better execution.

THE DOWNSIDE OF SHARING IS . . . NOTHING

Jessica Abel is a comic book artist, writer, and teacher — both online and in the classroom at the Pennsylvania Academy of Fine Arts, where she's the illustration chair.

Teaching everything that she knows is baked into who she is as a person. Her very first website in the 1990s was about creating your own comic book, and she has continued to teach others since then. With her current focus on launching creative ideas, she shares all of her expertise. Sharing has helped her own business build trust with her audience, assuring them that she's the person to come to for domain expertise.

As a classroom teacher, she knows that the first time she teaches a course can be a bit of a dog's breakfast — she will definitely make the material work and explain concepts to her students, but as questions and misunderstandings arise from this first round of teaching, she gets a very clear idea of what needs to be rewritten or rethought in her syllabus. So by teaching in the classroom, she receives essential feedback to make what she's teaching even stronger. In other words, she benefits just as much as her students do. She couldn't offer students a great class without teaching it the first time and then learning from their feedback.

Customer education — providing an audience with the knowledge, skills, and abilities to become an informed buyer — is one of the most important parts of a sales cycle. Too often we're so close to what we're selling that we assume others are also experts on it, or know what we know, but most of the time that's not the case. Customers don't always know what they don't know, or don't know enough about something to realize how useful or beneficial that information could be to them or their own business.

Companies in the past have not always been eager to invest in customer education, as they haven't seen clear or direct economic benefits from it. Conventional (but uninformed) wisdom has been that if you teach customers everything you know or share inside tricks of the trade, your customers will use that knowledge to not buy from you — or even worse, they'll buy from the competition instead, armed with the knowledge they gained from you. But these fears are just myths. In fact, the opposite tends to happen, according to a study done by Andreas Eisingerich and Simon Bell at the MIT Sloan School of Business.

Eisingerich and Bell surveyed 1,200 clients of an investment firm and found that the more those clients were educated on the pros and cons of the financial products the investment firm offered, the more they trusted that firm, the more loyalty to the firm they developed, and the more appreciative they became of the firm's customer service for taking the time to educate them.

The truth is that lots of companies use marketing ploys or disingenuous advertising to trick consumers into making a quick and sometimes impulsive decision. But these days, more and more consumers are demanding honest and straight information about products, so they can make their buying decisions at their own speed. By providing them with that kind of important knowledge, your company will form a strong link with customers, as you were the most helpful in their quest to learn before deciding.

Let me give you an example of how this works. Casper, a new breed of mattress company that's focused entirely on direct sales and internet marketing (similar to Need/Want), uses sleep education to indirectly sell its product. In the past, people who wanted to buy a mattress would go to a mattress store and test out several mattresses by lying on them, then choosing the one that felt the most comfortable. Since Casper's sales happen entirely online, the company decided to take a different, more education-focused approach, one that disrupts the traditional model for purchasing. Casper educates customers on why a solid night's sleep is important with two publications, "Van Winkles" and "Pillow Talk," which don't overtly sell mattresses and aren't littered with ads or purchase links. Rather, they convey everything Casper has learned about the science of sleep, which leads to greater consumer confidence in their brand. Combined with its superior-to-the-competition trial period — 100 percent full refund if not satisfied — Casper has been gaining market share without growing into retail stores or wholesale operations.

A company of one would be smart to follow this new trend of educating customers. Sharing vital information on a product or a service provides a new customer with key insights into how to use it and get the most out of it; you may even show people ways to use what you sell that they hadn't thought of. The lack of this kind of sharing can lead to customer frustration or distrust. They may even opt to buy a replacement product from someone else, all because they just didn't know how to properly use what they bought from you.

So, by sharing information about your product, you can help your customers or clients see why your company, based on all the information you've shared, will indeed be their best choice — and you'll be doing that without pushing that choice onto them.

Clearly, a major driver in all of this is the internet, which has democratized education. Businesses should take notice — customer education is the new form of marketing. Education makes a real difference between a product that people perfunctorily buy for utilitarian reasons and a product they are truly eager to purchase because it adds real purpose to their lives. As a company of one, what you teach people about your product can and will set you apart. So, for example, if you sell mailing list software, be sure to teach your clients about the importance of email marketing. If you sell sport bras, be sure to teach customers about fitness or the science of running. If you sell luggage, teach travel hacks.

TEACHING BUILDS AUTHORITY

If you're a company of one, asserting the authority of your own domain expertise becomes paramount, as there's nothing to hide behind. It's just you.

When it comes to selling and marketing, consumers are easily tempted to go with a larger company, which seems "safer" simply because it has more people and infrastructure to support it. Authority is the countermeasure to this instinct, as you can assuage any concerns from customers by making them feel that you are an authority on what you're selling. They'll trust that you have not only the answers but the right answer, one that will help them in a way that the competition, however big, cannot.

In other words, what we're talking about is creating an environment where customers respect and value your opinions because you've demonstrated consistent competency by educating them.

By building this type of authority, you can stand out in any industry because both your peers and customers turn to you for expertise, regardless of the size of your company. Word of mouth happens, Google links to you favorably, you're invited to speaking gigs, and so on — all because your expertise is valued. But how do you build authority? And how does it work?

If you think of the leaders in your industry, you can see that those people have an image of authority — like Debbie Millman in the field of graphic design, or Elon Musk in the field of electric cars. We look to these people for answers, we learn from them, and if we're part of the audience they're teaching, we probably buy from them as well.

In business these days, it's not enough to just tell people you're an authority — you've got to demonstrate your actual expertise by sharing what you know and teaching others. You build authority not by propping yourself up, but by teaching your audience and customers — so that they truly learn, understand, and succeed. When you make that happen consistently, you're building and establishing the right kind of authority.

Teaching your expertise positions you as an authority simply by virtue of the fact that you're showing someone else how to do something. People can be guarded if they think they're being sold to. But more often than not, customers will engage and open up if they feel like they're learning something useful. The more you teach, the more your audience will see you as an expert. Then, when it comes time to buy something, they'll find that they want to pay for more of that expertise. A study done in 2009 by neuroscientist Greg Berns at Emory University found that the decision-making centers of our brain slow down or shut off when we are receiving wanted advice from experts. Customers consistently rate experts as the most trusted spokespeople, far above typical CEOs or celebrities.

Basecamp has no internal goals or quotas around conversions or customer growth — its only mandate is to outshare and outteach everyone else by writing books, speaking at conferences, and even hosting workshops at the Chicago office. These events, called "The Basecamp Way to Work," share everything Basecamp has done to become a successful company, from internal communications to management organization. Nothing is held back or kept off the table. These $1,000 workshops sell out typically within minutes. Because of teaching what they know, and by showing others how they successfully run their company, they are the go-to experts for a tech company that isn't hell-bent on growth.

The reason these kinds of experts stand out, regardless of which industry they're in, is because they teach what they know. They share and give away their ideas freely. They don't worry about whether someone will steal their innovation for a product, a service, or a book — they just work at executing and sharing ideas faster and better than anyone else, in their own unique style and with their own unique personality. And this approach leads to business success.

Teaching builds trust and expertise like nothing else for a company of one. When someone's receptive to what you're teaching, they inherently trust the information you're sharing. If you can consistently give your audience useful, relevant, and timely knowledge (through your mailing list, speaking events, website, and so on), they'll begin to lean on you for more information (which you can then charge for). Teaching also doesn't require lots of time, resources, or even money—it can be as simple as sharing what you know with the people who are listening.

In sum, teach everything you know and don't be afraid to give away your best ideas.

BEGIN TO THINK ABOUT:

- What you could begin to share with or teach your customers or audience
- How you could focus more on executing ideas than on protecting them
- What investments you could make in consumer education as a marketing channel
- What you could share that would position you or your company as an authority in a niche

PART III

Maintain

10

■

Properly Utilizing
Trust and Scale

GLEN URBAN HAS BEEN STUDYING trust as it applies to consumers and businesses online for twenty years. The rise of the internet, making possible not only digital purchases but consumer reviews of those digital purchases, has given consumers a great deal of power.

Urban's research has consistently found that trust highly correlates to a person's propensity to consider, try, or buy a product. This finding predates the internet and goes back to family-run stores where one-to-one relationships were built; since these stores could be trusted to keep their promise to provide a good product at a fair price, purchases became multigenerational business transactions built on personal relationships. The internet has amplified these relationships and scaled them through the use of tools like social media, software, and newsletters. Trust, transparency, and communication are still absolutely required, but your relationships with customers can be scaled in a way that doesn't require scaling your business scale at the same time.

Urban found that the verified-purchase reviews that Amazon and eBay allow consumers to post help build trust when people want to learn more about products they might want to buy. While this review system can sometimes be "gamed" and companies can hire people to fill the hopper with good reviews, Amazon and eBay are constantly working to make sure that doesn't happen.

In some industries, like airlines and cell phone providers, trust either doesn't exist or is routinely broken. Cost pressure and consumer preference for the lowest price have forced these industries to cut costs to the bone, even to the detriment of how they treat their customers, which has created a huge lack of consumer trust.

Even wealth management services have been changed by the internet. As opinions and information are shared online, the model of high-pressure sales that prioritizes commissions over fund performance is being challenged by new robo-adviser services like WealthSimple. Traditional banks give 50 percent of their fee to a salesperson as a commission, but WealthSimple and similar robo-management services give bonuses to their advisers based solely on client feedback and happiness. Their fees are published on their websites for anyone to compare to other wealth management services they might wish to use.

Ellevest, a wealth management company that has built a new approach to women-focused investing (based on risk preferences, gender pay gaps, and women's longer life expectancy), has a fiduciary duty to act in their clients' best interests at all times and to not use their clients' assets for their own gain. Consumer trust increases when the ulterior motive of selling a product just to make a commission is removed from the transaction. This is why transparent companies like WealthSimple and Ellevest are rapidly acquiring new customers, without much churn.

Urban has found that trust is a strategy that starts before a product is even developed. A trust-based company of one begins with creating something that genuinely solves a problem; then the company rigorously tests the product's validity before honestly communicating its benefits and outcomes to customers. In this strategy, holding on to customers becomes more important than churning out old ones and constantly acquiring new ones.

Car dealers have a villainous reputation for pulling the wool over customers' eyes by doing everything from selling known "lemons" to altering odometers. In looking at the impact of the internet on car sales, Urban found that the internet has removed dealers' ability to scam customers by allowing them to share information like dealer invoices for car prices, safety ratings, VIN-based car reports, and even dealer reviews. You can now walk into a dealership knowing as much as, or more than, the person trying to sell you a new or used car.

When dealers found out that people were sharing this information, their first thought was to stop it by any means necessary — but the internet being what it is, they couldn't. Fast-forward to now, when car dealerships and salespeople mostly have embraced the new transparency and now work to get customers the right car for the right price. If they don't approach a sale in this way, customers will know (since they know what others have paid for similar cars) and they'll talk (by leaving poor reviews on rating websites). This is why some car manufacturers, like Mazda, now have fixed prices instead of negotiated prices, because if customers know what everyone else has paid for a car, they'll feel taken advantage of if they don't also get the lowest price. Everyone pays the same amount, and everyone is happy.

With the rise of consumer power from increased sharing and forced transparency, businesses have had to adapt to create win-win scenarios where they make a sale and keep the customer happy. But how do businesses balance trust and cost? Airlines, for one, won't be able to find this balance and grow trust until they become open about checked bags costing money, get rid of hidden fees, and never kick passengers off flights due to overbooking.

In studying how trust is built between companies and consumers, Urban has found that there are three aspects of trust: confidence ("I believe what you say"), competence ("I believe you have the skills to do what you say"), and benevolence ("I believe you're acting on my behalf"). He's found countless instances of companies that advocate for their customers. This is a long-term investment in honesty and transparency, and every company of one needs to employ it from the start.

TRUST BY PROXY

Why is this important to you and your company of one? Because the power of recommendation — or word of mouth — lies in its ability to create trust by proxy. If your good friend tells you that a product is worth buying, you'll listen because you trust your friend; some of that trust is then passed on to the product they're recommending. This works online to some degree as well: the people you follow have earned a bit of your trust, so you tend to trust their recommendations.

According to Nielsen, 92 percent of consumers trust recommendations from family or friends over any other form of advertising. The Word of Mouth Marketing Association found that a word-of-mouth conversation drives sales five times more than paid online media and is responsible for $6 trillion in annual customer spending. A study done by Verizon and Small Business Trends found that small business owners rated referrals and recommendations as their number-one way to acquire new customers, and that they greatly surpassed acquisition of new subscribers through search engines, social media, or paid ads.

So why isn't word-of-mouth marketing, or referral marketing, leaned on very often in businesses of any size? There are several reasons. Some businesses expect word of mouth to just happen organically, without any effort on their part. Another reason is the difficulty of measuring recommendations, which can happen via any medium from a coffee shop conversation to a private (untrackable) message on social media. Another reason businesses don't rely on referrals is that they're hard to quickly scale. That may be bad for a large business focused on exponential growth, but it's fine for a company of one. You don't need massive growth or scale to realize profits; since you can see benefits with much less mass, you can capitalize on products and consumer relationships that build referrals.

Companies of one can truly benefit from word of mouth because it's easier for a company of one to create these kinds of personal relationships and stay more closely connected with customers. Urban found that smaller businesses thrive on recommendations because they can focus solely on their specific audience and build relationships with them (even if they do that digitally). Small companies can take complaints and personally resolve them.

So how do you turn your customers into brand advocates and fuel conversations in which they share *your* business with the people they know? A study at Texas Tech found that while 83 percent of customers are willing to provide referrals, only 29 percent actually do so. For most businesses, this represents a huge missed opportunity to push happy customers to actively promote what you sell. Obviously, you need to have a good product with good customer service in place first; otherwise, no amount of incentives will create advocates for your product. In my own business, I doubled the amount of sharing for one of my products by automatically sending an email a week after purchase asking customers, if pleased with what they purchased, to share their satisfaction with others — using links with prewritten content provided.

A Harris Poll study conducted on behalf of Ambassador Software found that 88 percent of American consumers would like some kind of incentive to share products they like, and that number increases to 95 percent among eighteen- to thirty-five-year-olds. Incentives are another way to evangelize users, but they can be tricky. Sometimes offering cash incentives reduces trust if people find out that profit was the sole reason for promoting a product. Consumers are happy with incentives like small discounts, exclusive "swag," special offers, and access to premium features. They also like double-sided incentives: this is when both the referrer and the purchaser get a bit of a deal, such as, if I refer you to buy a rainbow widget, we both get $30 off our next order of rainbow widgets. Double-sided incentives have the bonus of increasing the likelihood of not one but two repeat sales.

Rewarding loyalty in your best customers is also a great way to incentivize recommendations. MailChimp is fairly well known for sending its loyal customers exclusive swag, like well-designed T-shirts (most don't even have the MailChimp logo on them) or "Freddie" action figures (Freddie is the name of the chimpanzee in the logo). People then post photos on social media — tagging MailChimp — that show them wearing their new shirt or the action figure on their desk, for all their followers to see.

Our friends at Ugmonk, whose story I told in Chapter 7, enjoy a great deal of word of mouth built on the quality of their products — Ugmonk shirts are so stylish that people want to share them on social media — as well as on the human touch in their customer service (they provide a replacement shirt, when necessary, without even asking the customer to return the original shirt). Founder Jeff Sheldon has seen the built-in virality of having a product that draws attention: the last time he was at an airport, three people stopped him to ask where he got the Ugmonk shirt he was wearing, with its distinctive designs. By focusing on slowly making his products better and more stylish for his niche audience, he's created a sustainable method of growth simply through referrals.

Referrals are also useful beyond the realm of products. Services and service-based companies of one (from consultants to freelancers to client-focused agencies) can greatly benefit from word of mouth. In fact, a survey done by Drip (an email service provider like MailChimp) found that 50 percent of new customers for service-based companies came from word of mouth. That survey result is definitely worth keeping in mind.

Where a service-based business can really capitalize on making word of mouth happen is by simply following up. Talking to clients a few weeks after a project is finished can yield two massive benefits. The first is being able to collect a testimonial or success story based on the real results the client is seeing. If you ask for a testimonial as soon as a project is finished, the client has rarely had enough time to collect any results-based data. By following up a few weeks or a few months later (depending on how long it will take to measure results), you can garner far better stories from clients to use in your marketing efforts. Second, by creating a schedule for following up with clients, you can then ask them (assuming the project went well) if they know of other businesses that could benefit from your services the way they have — or if they're interested in arranging another project with you. By creating a schedule for following up with contented clients, you can turn referrals into a real strategy instead of simply refreshing your inbox and hoping each day that one will come in.

Word of mouth can also be incentivized through the scalable system of segmented automation (as we saw in the previous chapter). For example, a week after a customer buys your product, you can generate an email asking them how much they're enjoying what they purchased from you on a scale of 1 to 10. Then a second email, which you would send only to people who rated their enjoyment above a 7, could pitch an incentive program, with a double-sided incentive and prewritten text to share on customers' social media feeds or in their own newsletters. For companies of one, focusing on existing and loyal customers as brand advocates — instead of trying to build an affiliate program of anyone who wants to make a quick buck referring you — creates a much greater trust, because those promoting your product already have a direct relationship with it. These are the customers who can tell the story of how they benefited from purchasing your product or service.

SEGMENTING TRUST

Unfortunately, a lot of people, especially creative people, look upon marketing in a negative way.

The truth is, they really shouldn't. Marketing is simply building a sense of trust and empathy with a specific group of people by consistently communicating with them. Trust has to be developed before anyone will buy anything. This is why ad-mail and cold-calling have such a tiny success rate and rely on massive volume — and conversely, why highly targeted cross-sell emails have a high success rate at a much smaller scale. For someone to want to buy your product, they have to feel that you understand their needs and have a solution for them. This isn't done through selling aimed at all people, but through consistent dialogue with a small and specific group of people. No company or product is too good to not have to consider and utilize marketing. No matter how great your product is, if you aren't reaching the right audience, you won't sustain your business.

Marketing is also no longer a silo job function within a larger organization — it's embedded in every role and aspect of a business, from customer support to product design. It's also not a single event — focused on a launch, for example. It's the sum total of everything your company does that a potential or actual customer sees or interacts with, from emails to casual conversations to tweets.

Where companies of one can use their focus on betterment over growth in marketing is by focusing on a specific niche instead of a massive market. Trust is more easily established within a smaller customer base because it's easier to stand out as an expert or to gather referrals that hold weight from other industry experts in that niche.

In recent years, large corporate business has focused its marketing and promotion efforts on collecting "vanity metrics" — like social media followers, subscribers, or clicks. But those metrics don't always correlate with sales, profit, or reputation. That is, they don't measure engagement or trust — they simply show how many people took some form of marketing bait. By considering "collecting" over "connecting" (with customers), these companies are becoming too caught up in collecting page likers and followers and have forgotten to build relationships with those individual customers who are already listening, following, or buying. Having 100 passionate fans of your business who are eager to buy anything you release is exponentially more effective than having 100,000 followers who simply follow your business to win something like a free iPad.

Making money is often easier than earning trust, because money can be lost and won back without judgment, whereas trust is hard to regain once it's lost. Your word and your company's word have to be a contract with your customers. This is how many companies of one stand out in competitive industries: by simply doing the work they say they'll do and then honoring social contracts with their customers. Even a big company like Amazon has services built on trust. First it was the promise to deliver in less than seven days. Then they went to two-day delivery. Now, in some places (not in the woods, or on an island), Amazon delivers on the same day. We buy from Amazon because we trust that our order will be delivered quickly, and that, if we aren't happy, it will be easy to return. So trust happens first. Only then does the commerce follow.

In trust marketing, a group of people trusts you enough to invest their personal attention, email address, or dollars with your company. This kind of marketing requires that you always keep the promises you make and engage in a consistent dialogue with them.

While it may seem counterintuitive to focus your marketing and trust-building efforts on a small and specific group of people, there are benefits to doing so. The more specific you are with who your products or services are for, the more you can build trust with that particular audience. The paradox of focusing on a niche is that the more specific you are, the easier it is to sell to that group and the more likely it is that you can charge a premium for being that focused. With that kind of focus in mind, you can get to know the specifics of your niche better, learn how to serve customers more effectively, and build a reputation for yourself in that smaller niche.

Kurt Elster, instead of spending his time building an audience for general ecommerce consulting services, focuses entirely on Shopify store owners. (More than 400,000 businesses use Shopify as an ecommerce platform.) By using this niche to build trust in a smaller and more specific audience, Kurt has grown his revenue eightfold and made a name for himself as an authority in Shopify consulting; he was even featured on Shopify's website. His reputation for helping Shopify store owners has, in turn, brought him more leads, allowed him to set higher prices for his services, and helped him land speaking gigs around the world. If you had a Shopify store, whom would you trust with your business — a general ecommerce consultant or someone like Kurt who focuses only on Shopify?

TRUST DOESN'T REQUIRE
A BIG BUDGET

By making customer happiness your top priority over new customer acquisition and then incentivizing customers to share the word about your business, less of your money needs to be spent on promotion. With a company of one, which can be profitable at any size, such slow but sustainable growth makes sense. You start with the idea of creating a trust-centric business, build products that customers love, make sure they're educated and happy with what they've purchased from you, and then give them systematic ways to share their success with others.

This doesn't require huge billboards, massive ad spends, or paid acquisitions. In treating trust as a primary factor in running your business, you'll amass an army of loyal fans — and not just a huge customer base of people who bought from you and then forgot about you.

The truth is, you don't need Super Bowl ads. Instead, as a company of one, you can be more effective by writing guest articles for websites and blogs, creating incentive programs for existing clients, or appearing in podcasts that cover your industry.

Alex Beauchamp, former head of content at Airbnb, said that she never wants any content she works on to "go viral." She doesn't want to ever be on the hook for making that happen. Moreover, going viral is often what happens with a business that, not understanding who its intended audience is, tries to appeal to pretty much everyone. If you want a piece of content for your business to generate a billion views, you probably don't understand the purpose of that content or whom it was really created for. Engagement and connection with your niche are more important and far less costly to generate.

Alex, in her current role as director of content at Edmonds.com, knows that trust is more important than virality when it comes to content. As an objective third-party review website for cars, Edmonds.com can't appear partial to any one car brand by taking ads or sponsored content. That would immediately ruin trust with its specific audience. So instead, Alex and her team create impartial reviews, based on the merits of each vehicle, that are intended for the specific audience of engaged car-buyers. She says that the best platform is the one you've already got — by catering to people who are already listening and focusing on them, you can draw in others as well.

As noted earlier, education is a better and cheaper way to build your customer base. When you teach customers about how products like yours can be used or can benefit their own businesses or lives, trust is the natural outcome. BoatUS, a company that provides insurance and tows for water vehicles, uses education for customers and noncustomers alike with its mobile phone app that features water hazard warnings and tide charts — for free. If your business becomes a source of information, you're giving your customers what they need to make their own informed decision (even if they decide not to buy from your business). This type of education, like a free resource page on your website or a small but free mobile app, can be a cost-effective way to promote both your products and customers' trust in them.

Jason Fried told me that Basecamp recently flirted with paid acquisition by spending around $1 million on social media ads. They quickly stopped because they found that these ads weren't as effective as what they were doing already: creating and sharing educational content. For instance, in the absence of any acquisition or paid ads, over 4,400 people signed up for their software in one week alone. They decided to focus on a great product, amazing customer service, and incentivizing existing customers with referral bonuses. Jason said that he would rather give money to his happy customers to bring in more customers through incentives than buy ads from big businesses like Facebook or Google. It costs them a lot less money as well.

There's no reason to compete with highly expensive ad spends to gain customers; moreover, such campaigns are especially difficult for a company of one, because of the scale that's required and, of course, the cost. Let me give you a perfect example that is close to home for me.

The Pointe Restaurant in Tofino is an award-winning, high-end dining experience (and my favorite place to eat). They greet you with a glass of champagne, and the waitstaff then gets to know you a bit as they bring you five to seven immaculately prepared courses over several hours. The chef tends to make an appearance to see how the night is going. When the bill arrives, the maitre d' asks if you'd like your car brought around to the front. While the food obviously backs up the restaurant's top-of-the-line status, the personal touches are what set it apart and make it a luxury brand that people talk about. The personal touches may not cost much more to implement (for example, hiring waitstaff who make the effort to get to know people), but surprising and delighting customers can go a long way toward building trust. And with service like this, they can charge a huge premium.

Trust in business is more than a matter of adopting an internal slogan or making up a mantra to apply to products and services when it suits a marketing campaign. Trust has to be totally baked into every aspect of not only what you sell, but how you sell and support it. For a company of one, even at a tiny scale, maintaining a business worthy of customer trust creates a market differentiator and helps you stand out. Such a business focuses on quality over speed, compassion over profit, and honesty over tricks. And since, as a customer, you certainly prefer to buy from trusted businesses, why change that when you're the one doing the selling?

BEGIN TO THINK ABOUT:

- How you embed trust and honesty as a marketing strategy in your company of one
- The relationships you could foster with your customers to incentivize them to share word of your business with others
- How to ensure — whether through email, support, or social media — that you're always honoring social contracts with your customers

11

■

Launching and Iterating in Tiny Steps

I KNOW I HAVE TALKED ABOUT Ugmonk a couple of times earlier in the book, but it's such a fascinating and inspirational story of how a company of one got started that I want to return to it one more time and provide some more detail on how it began. A month after Ugmonk founder and creator Jeff Sheldon graduated from college, in 2008, he married his high school sweetheart and moved to Burlington, Vermont, to start a full-time job at a design agency. He was enamored with minimal design and typography, but couldn't find clothing that matched this aesthetic. He started with just one idea and four T-shirt designs.

But instead of planning a large clothing company, with factories, warehouses, and supply chains for large retailers, Jeff began with a $2,000 loan from his father and a plan to be profitable as quickly as possible — by outsourcing production to American T-shirt printers. (He carefully selects every manufacturing company he works with for both quality and alignment with his ethics.)

Because he started with just four designs and a tiny run of 200 shirts, after paying back the small loan, Jeff was able to be profitable almost instantly. Only when the first, then the second, then the third run of his T-shirts quickly sold out did he increase his costs by ordering more inventory. By working to become profitable as quickly as possible in tiny steps and not waiting for tremendous scale to happen, Jeff got a bonus: scale happened anyway. In short, his profits rose because the increased volume cut his costs. While growing this way wasn't Jeff's initial plan, it served him well by letting him figure out how to make money at a small scale first, then grow iteratively, based on customer demand.

For two years Jeff created clothing and routinely sold it out through Ugmonk and its website while still working in his full-time design job. He worked nights and weekends building Ugmonk, refining designs, organizing logistics, and packing orders. During those first two years he lived off his salary from the full-time job and invested all the profits from Ugmonk back into his company of one until there was enough momentum and scale to pay himself and the other people who worked with him. It wasn't until his first tiny apartment became too crammed full of inventory that he moved to a larger warehouse and fulfillment center.

Although Ugmonk was profitable from the beginning, Jeff has been careful not to scale too quickly. He moves slowly, iterating in small steps, slowly increasing production, the number of products, and what the company takes on. Like Need/Want from Chapter 8, Ugmonk still sells directly to customers, as it requires less staff and resources. And because Ugmonk has always been focused on the quality of both its designs and its products, they routinely get free press from design publications and blogs.

MINIMUM VIABLE PROFIT

As a company of one, you need to reach profitability as quickly as possible. Since you're not relying on massive influxes of cash from investors, every minute you spend getting set up and started is a minute when you aren't making money. So getting your product or service released as soon as possible, even if it's small, is both financially wise and educational, since a quick release can also serve as a perfect learning experience. The first version of a product doesn't need to be huge — it simply needs to solve one problem well and leave your customers feeling better than before they purchased it.

In determining your minimum viable profit — the point at which your business is operating in the black (we'll call it MVPr from here on in) — keep in mind that the lower the number, the quicker you can reach it. So it's important to scale up your timelines and focus on core features only, reduce expenses and overhead, and ensure that your business model works at a small scale first.

The assumption at work here is that your MVPr — not the number of your customers, not your measured growth, not even your gross revenue — is the most important determinant of the sustainability of your company of one. If you make a profit right from the beginning, then you can figure out everything else. If your expenses are low, profit happens sooner. Decisions should be made with a focus on realized profit, not based on the expectation that profit may happen. This is such a key and main difference in how growth-focused businesses and companies of one operate. Even when a company of one needs to grow, that can happen only if metrics are based on actual profit, not on hopeful profit projections.

Your MVPr can be low in the beginning, as companies of one typically start with either just one person or a tiny team of two to three people with the abilities and skills to create what needs creating. These teams get larger only if more people are truly needed and if profits can support them. Profit happens when the business is making enough money to cover a salary for the owner(s); this is the "minimum" part of MVPr, as a company of one can be a full-time endeavor only when it's making enough to support at least one person. Viability is when MVPr either continues to support that one person long-term or increases with time. The more viable your company becomes, the more your profits can truly grow. From there, you can choose to pay yourself more, to focus on scaling systems, to work less and keep paying yourself the same, to invest in the business further, or to grow based on the increased money coming in. In the end, the choice is yours.

Becoming a business that earns revenues predictably and consistently is a milestone for a company of one. MVPr is achieved with the least investment and in the shortest amount of time possible.

Quickly becoming profitable is important to a company of one because focusing on growth and focusing on profit are nearly impossible to do at the same time. For big companies, traditional growth requires investing in the future, and that usually means spending money on a sales cycle with the bet that it will pay off at a higher rate . . . *sometime in the future.* A focus on growth may require spending money on sales staff, paid acquisitions, increased support teams, or even a larger technology infrastructure to handle the hoped-for growth. The assumption is that, eventually, more spending will generate more profit.

Focusing on profit down the road doesn't work for a company of one. A company of one begins quite small (one person, no office required) and spends only when profits allow it. Growth is much slower because it's incremental from zero — a tiny amount of profit leads to a tiny amount of spending, which leads to slightly more profit and then slightly more spending, and so on. It's a very gradual process.

With companies of one, exponential profit increases aren't a core objective because just hitting profitability is usually enough. From there, you have choices — to grow, to stay the same, to take more time off, to scale systems — as well as the space to make those choices because your goal isn't to make exponential profit, but simply to bring in profits greater than your expenses.

SIMPLICITY SELLS (QUICKLY)

According to entrepreneur and author Dan Norris, you don't learn anything until you launch.

It might sound obvious, but a product is built to solve a specific problem. But as Dan points out, you won't know how well your product solves that problem until people are actually paying for it and using it. Whether you're selling cars, accounting software, or falafels from a falafel stand, these products exist to fix or address an existing and pressing problem. You can travel great distances quickly having a vehicle that goes much faster than walking. Keeping track of expenses and sales is important to every business—doing it with automated software beats using scrap paper. And falafels? They solve hunger (or guilty pleasure cravings).

Every minute you spend as a company of one in the ongoing development of a new product is a minute you aren't seeing how well it solves a problem, and even worse, you aren't making money from it or building toward your MVPr. That's why getting a working version of your product released as quickly as possible is important: your company needs to start generating cash flow and obtaining customer feedback. Andrew Mason founded Groupon as a basic website where he manually typed in deals and created PDFs to email to subscribers from Apple Mail. Pebble, a smartwatch, started with just a single explainer video and a Kickstarter campaign (no actual product, even) that raised more than $20 million to fund its development; Pebble was eventually sold to FitBit. Virgin started as a single Boeing 747 flying between Gatwick, England, and Newark, New Jersey.

Once these startups were up and running, they were able to build from customer feedback and make positive changes.

In much the same way, companies of one need to continually

iterate on their products to keep them useful, fresh, and relevant to the market they serve. So, launch your company quickly, but then immediately start to refine your product and make it better. When you launch a first version of a product, you're guessing at a lot of things — how it's positioned in its market, how easy or difficult it will be to reach your target audience and get its attention, and how willing people will be to buy it and at what price. But the good news is that once you launch the first version, data immediately starts to pour in. How are sales going? How are the reviews? How is customer retention? Are they so excited about your product that they are telling others? You can and must use this data to further refine your product to be an even better and more useful solution to the problem you set out to solve.

I can't emphasize this point enough: finding a simple solution to a big or complicated problem is your strongest asset as a company of one. Your unique ingenuity can't be outsourced to artificial intelligence or to a massive team. Your ability to problem-solve with simplicity will keep you and your skills relevant in any market. The benefit of starting small is that you can start with only a few customers using your product and you can speak to them directly — for feedback, suggestions, and improvements.

For a company of one to launch a new product, the process has to be simple. (If you recall from Chapter 1, this is a defining trait of companies of one.) Your launch should be simple in choice, simple in messaging, and simple in hypertargeting only one audience.

There are three elements to the psychology of simple, according to Harvard professor George Whitesides: predictability, accessibility, and serving as a building block. Being predictable means that simple products are easy to instantly understand. A product that solves a single problem, like a Casper mattress helping you get a good night's sleep, is simple. Casper doesn't make 108 styles of mattresses, they make three. Being accessible means being honest: Casper makes no over-the-top claims, but backs its product with solid research and overwhelmingly positive reviews from over 400,000 customers.

Finally, to serve as a building block is to build on an existing and understood concept. Casper didn't invent a soft and rectangular piece of foam to sleep on and call it a mattress. They simply built off an existing industry, an existing product, and made it better. Everyone knows what a mattress is, so Casper doesn't have to explain that; they just have to explain *why* their mattress is better. In effect, Casper doesn't market mattresses but rather *better sleep,* with their mattresses being a means to that end. They're consistent in this message across all media (social media, their blog, and any other advertising). The hyperfocused target market for a Casper mattress is younger people who are ready to upgrade their lumpy mattress but hate going to stores and talking to salespeople. These are the customers who'd rather buy on line, with a guarantee that if they don't like the product, they can return it (after 100 nights' sleep).

Keeping your launch simple lets you avoid roadblocks in getting your product to market and then sharing it with the market. If it's not simple, you'll have to spend too much time first creating your product, and then explaining what it is and what it does. Simple lets you hit MVPr sooner and really start learning how your product is faring in the market.

FUNDING YOUR OWN PRODUCTS, VCS NOT REQUIRED

Let's return to Ugmonk's Jeff Sheldon, who wanted to create and sell a desk organizer called Gather. Selling physical products can be tough, as they involve a great deal of prior planning and then manufacturing agreements that can involve minimum orders and therefore large investments of upfront cash. This is why many product companies go after funding or bank loans or require a massive amount of capital to begin.

Not so with Gather, however: Jeff decided to test his idea for his new product by creating a crowdfunding campaign for it. This approach, he felt, would see how much his audience wanted Gather; if they did, they would raise the capital he needed to build it without the need to give up control to investors. And because he'd already spent a decade building an audience that was ravenous for his Ugmonk brand, Jeff's Kickstarter campaign was able to generate over $430,000 (surpassing his original funding goal by 2,394 percent), garnering him more than enough to cover all the costs required to put Gather into production.

Jeff was now able to ramp up production to an existing audience for this product, and he got funding directly from that audience instead of from outside investors who might not have completely shared his vision. As mentioned earlier, the Pebble watch, one of the first smartwatches created, would not have even gotten off the ground if it hadn't been for their crowdfunding efforts — which quickly became the most-funded Kickstarter project ever. (Even raising over $20 million from 78,471 backers, however, didn't ensure Pebble's long-term success.)

Not surprisingly, crowdfunding, as an alternative to raising capital from investors, is a growing trend in new businesses. It's far easier to access than VC money, and it puts your idea directly into the hands of potential customers — if they agree with your idea, they'll pledge money as a preorder. If they don't, you'll only have wasted time developing the crowdfunding campaign (the marketing and possibly prototypes), not months or years in product development.

It's not as cut and dry, though, as "VC = bad, crowdfunding = good." VC money can sometimes come with much-needed mentorship and even the required connections on which to build business relationships. Capital can also come with the business experience needed not only to create a product but also to run a company. It's just often very tricky to find investors. As any entrepreneur will tell you, people who have money and who share your vision and are eager to invest in your idea are often hard to find.

While VCs are interested in their own profits and partial ownership of their investments, crowdfunding seems more aligned with companies of one — if the product idea solves a problem for an audience, that audience will become customers. Profit will be generated quickly and at the outset, allowing you to make choices about your business and how it will proceed based entirely on the money it's making. If your crowdfunding is done right, it can be extremely beneficial, but bear in mind that crowdfunding isn't always a surefire way to raise money: typically, only 35 percent of Kickstarter campaigns are successfully funded. Nevertheless, though crowdfunding is still a niche, it was responsible for about $6 billion in money raised in 2016. Olav Sorenson, professor of management at Yale University, believes that crowdfunding is best suited for consumer-facing products, and not as likely to succeed for business-focused products.

Crowdfunding is also a little more meritocratic than traditional ways of raising capital. Research from Harvard Business School shows that investors — who are predominantly white males — prefer ventures pitched and run by people like themselves, i.e., other white men. By contrast, women excel with crowdfunding, according to research from PwC and the Crowdfunding Center: they are actually 32 percent more successful at hitting their fundraising goals than men.

Consider the case of Katherine Krug, the CEO of a company called BetterBack, which has raised more than $3 million in crowdfunding for its devices that help anyone with lower-back issues from sitting at a desk. With no outside investments influencing her, she's able to completely control the direction of her company. Katherine, who famously turned down a *Shark Tank* deal, believes that crowdfunding is an ideal platform for female entrepreneurs to secure the capital needed to develop new products. She's also found that crowdfunding is more liberating for companies of one, as too many VCs tend to consider $500,000 or even $1 million companies just too small to invest in. BetterBack operates without an office and with a small team spread around the globe. Katherine herself works from various parts of the world, spending each quarter in a different country. Her business, and how she leads her employees, are more focused on personal growth than on exponential profit increases.

CAPITAL ISN'T ALWAYS REQUIRED

Sometimes, if your idea for a business or product requires a substantial influx of funds to start, it could be that your idea is too large or too complex. And sometimes you should start a business only when people are asking you for something and are willing to give you money for it.

Derek Sivers began CDBaby—which sold for $22 million in 2008, while it was doing approximately $250,000 a month in net profit—by accident when he began selling his own band's CDs on the internet. Friends asked if he could sell their albums for them as well, and as more people asked, a revenue model began to form and Derek's CDBaby business was born. But in the beginning, it required no capital to start—just an idea and the time it took to execute it well.

CDBaby never took on investors, even though there were weekly offers from outsiders who wanted to invest. Derek didn't need CDBaby to expand quickly because it was profitable from the start and it focused on serving its audience, not expanding its own profit margins. He didn't have to please anyone but his customers and himself. Every decision, he feels, whether it's to raise money, to expand a business, or to run promotions, should be done according to what's best for your customers. Derek spent $500 to start CDBaby, made $300 in his first month and $700 in the second, and was profitable from that point on.

Customers typically don't ask a business to grow or expand. If growth isn't what's best for them, maybe it should be reconsidered. Because when you do focus primarily on your customers and their satisfaction, as we saw in Chapter 7, they'll tell everyone about you.

Crew, back in Chapter 3, started with a one-page website and a form to collect information in order to manually match freelancers to businesses. When the demand became too large to handle manually, they invested in building custom software. When they launched another product, Unsplash (royalty-free stock photographs), they did so in a similar manner: they bought a $19 Tumblr theme and uploaded ten high-resolution images taken by a local photographer. Within three hours, the first low-fi version was launched. They did the work manually until a scalable system was absolutely required, then invested in it with their profits. Now, a few years later, more than 1 billion photos are viewed per month through Unsplash (and it's now a profitable business, although it is VC-backed at this point).

This may sound obvious, but businesses need to solve problems for their customers. Whether it's selling a mattress that helps customers get a better night's sleep or stock photographs, a business succeeds only when it's viewed by your audience as useful. So your first goal, as a company of one just starting out, is to figure out the best way to solve a specific audience's problems, and then get to work at doing it quickly and cost-effectively.

By starting out small, a company of one can put all of its energy into solving problems for real people rather than into growing large enough to *maybe* solve problems for people one day. This approach also gives your relationship with customers a strong foundation: by eliminating bureaucracy and the friction of large infrastructures, you can interact with, listen to, and empathize with your customers directly.

For example, if you'd like to sell an online course that teaches people how to run an online business, then it's faster to offer that advice as a one-on-one consulting service first. That way you don't need to wait to turn a profit until you've filmed all the videos, developed or set up an online course platform, and built the audience required to make money from online courses. Profit can happen as soon as you get your first customer paying you for individual instruction.

Halley Gray, founder of Evolve + Succeed, has found that most people who start a new business by themselves make the mistake of believing the products should always come first. Instead of developing a product, which can take a lot of time (and sometimes cash) to develop, new founders can start almost immediately by offering their product idea as a service first. This is what Danielle LaPorte did with her "Fire Starter Sessions" after she was fired from the company she founded and then went out on her own. By offering services first, she was able to generate income almost immediately, as well as prove that there was a market for her products when her one-on-one service-based work took off. By doing this, she learned a great deal about her audience and determined what they wanted from her, so when her products were launched, they sold very well and her million-dollar-plus business was born.

LAUNCH QUICKLY — AND LAUNCH OFTEN

Too often we believe that we get only one chance to launch a product or a business, that the first splash is all that matters. If it doesn't become massively profitable right away, we think, then it's doomed. We somehow feel that there's magic in the first time we open our (sometimes digital) doors to the public.

The problem with this thinking is that most launches *aren't* massive successes. Yes, they can be slightly profitable (if everything goes right), but often things don't pay off as quickly as we hoped, because we're still mostly guessing in the beginning. We guess at the intended audience, the positioning of the product, and the value that audience will assign to what we're selling. WD-40, the well-known everyday lubricant, is literally named after its thirty-nine failures and one success. Originally it was created for the aerospace industry, but it became so popular with employees using it for other tasks that it was brought to retail, where it thrived. GM launched an electric car (the EV-1) in 1996, but found it was too "niche" and scrapped the program; twenty years later, in 2017, their Chevrolet Bolt (also an electric car) was the *Motor Trends* Car of the Year. Only after you've first launched can you then start to measure data and collect key insights: what worked, what did not, how was it received, and how could it be positioned differently?

Launching isn't a onetime, singular event, but a continual process of launch, measure, adjust, repeat. The cofounder of LinkedIn, Reid Hoffman, has said that if you aren't embarrassed by the first version of your product, you've launched too late. It's ridiculous to believe that every company grows out of a founder's fully formed and unchanging idea, especially since most wildly successful companies achieved their place only by course-correcting, changing entirely, or iterating their way to greatness.

Jim Collins, best-selling author of *Good to Great*, studied 1,435 companies over a forty-year span. He found that every great company that's very profitable and successful started out as simply good enough to launch. These companies focused on one thing and let go of the rest. He likens it to foxes and hedgehogs. Foxes are very smart and wily and have many tricks for catching prey.

In contrast, a hedgehog has only a single trick — curling up into a spike-laden ball. Regardless of how many tricks a fox deploys to catch a hedgehog, the hedgehog's singular trick beats all of them, because a fox can't eat a hedgehog. Many companies try to be foxes, doing everything for everyone or launching products full of bells and whistles, but successful companies that thrive over the long term work at a single task and master it. You still need a varied skill set to build a company of one, but your focus on serving customers needs to be singular.

This singular focus is made far easier with today's technology. "Every company now is a technology company," says Anil Dash. In the past it made sense to separate out tech companies from all others, but now every company, even a company of one, relies heavily on technology. From their use of email to ecommerce software to automation in manufacturing, every company is now a tech company, with technology at its disposal, not just to create the scalable systems we spoke about in Chapter 8, but to enable further focus. For example, a company doesn't need to put its efforts into developing a new online payment system; it can use Stripe, Square, or PayPal instead. A company doesn't need to invest time and resources in building a content management system for its website; it can use WordPress. Streaming video required? Just use YouTube. Looking for supply chain management? There are now hundreds of software solutions. By using existing technology to run as much of a business as possible, you can better focus on your core idea — the core solution — and find your core niche.

Because the first launch generally doesn't yield amazing results, companies of one should try to get it out of the way as soon as they have something to launch. Then the focus can turn to making the product better, based on what was learned. By iterating and relaunching, greater results can be achieved. Companies of one need to continually iterate on their products to keep them useful and relevant to the market they're intended to serve. So launch quickly, but immediately start to refine and improve your product.

Iterating is an ongoing process, by the way, and should never stop as long as you're receiving feedback and data from the market, from other businesses in your niche, and even from within your organization (such as requests from the support person or team). Your strategy, then, shouldn't be rigid and set in stone, but capable of being changed each time new information is collected. In this way, your strategy will never fall out of sync with the customers and market you're serving.

Blockbuster failed to iterate to the changing market and Netflix slaughtered its profits. To quote Blockbuster's CEO in an interview with *Motley Fool*: "Neither RedBox nor Netflix are even on the radar screen in terms of competition," he said. Blockbuster ended up with hopelessly outdated retail stores, which led to huge overhead and debt and then bankruptcy. When Sears failed to change its practice of putting catalogs in every home, it lost out to Walmart and Amazon. In 2006, Ed Zander, CEO of Motorola, said this about the Apple iPod Nano: "Screw the Nano. What the hell does the Nano do? Who listens to 1,000 songs?" In 1946, Darryl Zanuck, the cofounder of 20th Century Fox, said, "Television won't be able to hold onto any market it captures after the first six months. People will soon get tired of staring at a plywood box every night." Without iteration and adjustment based on new data and insights, a company will stagnate and die.

But if you've launched, once or several times, and it hasn't resulted in enough profit to sustain even a single person's cost of living, how do you know when to stay resilient and push on — and how do you know when to pack it in and quit (that is, when to move on to a brand-new idea or business)?

That was the question that best-selling author Tim Ferriss, on his podcast, asked Scott Belsky, the cofounder of Behance, an online portfolio platform for creatives. Scott feels that whether we find that line between stubbornly proceeding when we shouldn't and resiliently persevering when we should has to do with the truth of our initial assumption. In other words, if you're at a place where you aren't sure what to do because things haven't worked out, do you still think that your initial assumption was correct? And in knowing all you know at this point, would you pursue the project all over again?

If the answer is yes, if you still think your original idea was valid, can be profitable in some way, and is worth pursuing, you should carry on. If not, if you're continuing only because you've put so much of your time and energy and heart into the project, then it's not logical to keep at it. If you're overvaluing your plan because it's your plan (known as the "endowment effect"), then you should probably quit.

The idea that winners never quit is both overly simplistic and completely false. Most successful founders of companies have quit several times. In fact, it's their quitting that led them to the success they found after they failed. In his 1937 book *Think and Grow Rich,* Napoleon Hill said, "A quitter never wins and a winner never quits," but that just doesn't hold true. Sony's founder, Akio Morita, first invented a rice cooker that burned rice (a fairly good reason to quit). Ev Williams founded, then quit, a podcasting platform named Odeo (which Apple made obsolete when it launched its own podcasting platform soon after). Williams then moved on to found Twitter and Medium.

So if you have refused to change anything because of your misaligned ownership of an idea and because of all that you've invested (time, money, resources), then yes, you may be continuing for the wrong reasons. But if your initial vision still seems objectively valid and progress and profit are just coming along slower than you'd like, by all means continue.

In the early days of Behance, Scott Belsky and his small team were just a few months away from completely running out of money. Understandably, they felt demotivated quite often, but their vision of organizing the creative world's work never got less interesting or less valuable to their customers. So while they tired sometimes of soldiering on without enjoying massive success, they didn't lose their original conviction. When things got really tough, they became even more resilient — they found ways to create scalable systems and repurposed work instead of spending money on new hires. They reduced costs to a minimum so they could achieve profit faster. Even today, when Behance is popular (more than 60 million views of projects per month) and owned by Adobe, the design team responsible for all of Behance's visual creations and its publication 99U (print, digital, and a series of conferences) is a staggeringly tiny staff of just three people.

So, by working toward MVPr as quickly as possible with a simple solution and then iterating upon it after it's launched, your company of one can build a resilient business that may change over time in its products or features, but still serves and is totally valuable to its customers.

BEGIN TO THINK ABOUT:

- A new business or product you could start right now by executing the smallest version of your idea
- How to determine your MVPr, the steps that could be taken to achieve it as quickly as possible, and what could be scaled back to reach it faster
- A product or service that would be the simplest solution to a problem your customers are having
- Whether you could start your company of one without capital and what that would look like

12

∎

The Hidden Value
of Relationships

CHRIS BROGAN, THE *New York Times* best-selling author and CEO of Owner Media Group, doesn't believe in hustling. Instead, he'd rather build long-term relationships with people based on mutually shared interests.

Chris believes that smaller business owners (and companies of one) are sometimes embarrassed about selling, and have an aversion to it, because they believe that selling means pushing your products on others. What he and many others have found, though, is that it's much easier to sell to people with whom you've already built a relationship because they know that you actually care about them personally and their betterment. In this kind of relationship, selling doesn't have to be pushy. It's based entirely on a cultivated friendship.

On the flip side, if your business is constantly selling and constantly pushing its wares, people instinctively start to avoid your business or stop responding to your emails. But if you use your platform to teach, empower, and make customers' lives or businesses better (as we saw in Chapter 9), you are seen as a trusted adviser, not a shady or slick salesperson. This is why Chris promotes friends and people he finds who are doing interesting work, without being asked to. He creates relationships by constantly thinking: *Who do I know who could benefit from connect-*

ing with this person? Then he facilitates those connections, either one-on-one or by sharing with his entire audience. Over time this unique approach creates a lot of goodwill with others and with his audience, which helps when Chris himself has something to pitch or to sell.

Chris feels that these kinds of relationships can help companies of one because consumers innately trust smaller businesses over large corporations, deservedly or not. There's a huge difference, Chris says, between "How are you, Cleveland, Ohio?" and "How are you, Paul Jarvis?" Companies of one can use this personalized approach to their advantage by calling out customers by name or speaking to them directly. For example, if you have a mailing list of 1,000 people and most of them reply to your newsletters, you'll be able to read and personally reply to each one. Large corporations just aren't set up to do that kind of personal outreach.

Smaller businesses tend to want to act like larger companies, which is curious, since many large businesses these days are trying to act like smaller ones. Chris has noticed a trend, especially in the realm of food and beverages: consumer demand for better-quality food (at a higher price) has driven large brands to either acquire or act like smaller artisanal companies. For example, Anheuser-Busch owns at least ten craft beer companies. The office supply store Staples, seeing that people have become less and less likely to visit its retail locations, launched a campaign called "Summon Your Inner Pro," which focuses instead on cultivating business-to-business relationships. When customers say that they want more personal experiences from a brand, what they really want is a more personal connection or relationship with the company, so as to be understood better by them.

Chris believes that small businesses need to start embracing and acting like small businesses. Companies of one can be proud to be companies of one and can use their personality to stand out and their smaller focus to niche down to the specific groups of customers they want to serve. They can know customers by name, by need, and by motivation. Nurturing a relationship with customers ultimately reduces the likelihood of their going elsewhere and also strengthens their belief that smaller can be better.

Where some businesses (of any size) get relationships wrong, Chris says, is in laying claim to ownership of their audience, using phrases like "our audience." While this might seem a trivial point, it's an important one, because no audience or consumer group is solely one business's property. You can't own an audience, because they support, buy from, and enjoy many other products from companies besides your own. They rarely think 24/7 *just* about your business.

Implied in community ownership is a company's assumption that it's okay to use that relationship to sell them more. That kind of mentality can easily turn an audience or community against a company. This is why Chris uses his own mailing list mostly just to connect with his audience, through weekly articles; (very) occasionally, he pitches them products he's created. For the most part, though, he uses his list to connect with the community he serves with news, information, and valuable content. Building relationships by being helpful first enables an audience to benefit from the relationship, and that experience will lead them to feel a sense of real reciprocity later when you try to sell them something.

THE TRUE NORTH OF
AUDIENCE-BUILDING

You can't buy your way into real relationships any more than you can force people to buy your products. To create an audience of people who are keen to support your business by purchasing from you, a real relationship is required first — one that includes trust, humanity, and empathy.

Building a genuine audience around your business, product, or brand is not the same as growth-hacking. In fact, the overall concept of this entire book is antithetical to that practice.

Companies of one don't growth-hack, because the true north of growth-hacking is, of course, growth. Growth to growth-hacking companies is the single metric used to gauge validity or success, and thinking of it as always beneficial (which, as we've learned from the countless stories and research studies reported in previous chapters, is untrue), they consider it not only useful but entirely necessary. Relationships for growth-hackers mostly revolve around offsetting churn, in that their goal is to build an audience as quickly as possible, then sell as much as possible to them until they relent, buy, or give up and leave. This "churn and burn" mentality can lead to faster short-term profits (or at least short-term audience growth), but it has nothing to do with relationship building—and it mostly involves paid acquisition. "Churn and burn" doesn't create or foster personal connections, and it isn't based on trust or shared interests. It's simply a way to work toward a scale at which profit can happen for a growth-focused business.

Glide, a video chat app, launched at number one in the social networking section of Apple's app store, mostly owing to the viral nature of its invitation system. By default, the app scrapes a user's address book and spamvites via text message everyone in your contacts. (A spamvite is like an invitation, but one you didn't knowingly send.) This happens by default when you start using Glide's app; to keep the app from texting your entire contact list, you have to find the right setting to turn it off. After a lot of negative press and pushback, Glide said that it had changed its "growth strategy" away from spamviting customers' entire address books, but in reality, it was still happening years later. Glide has since dropped hundreds of spots in the social networking section of Apple's app store.

The Circle, another app that focused on growth-hacking, spam-blasted its customers' contact lists in hopes of gaining faster growth. CEO Evan Reas later changed his view on growth-hacking after it repeatedly backfired for his company; he came to believe that a business should grow as the result of great customer experience, not just grow for the sake of growing while taking away from great customer experience. Andy Johns, head of Product at Wealthfront (formerly at Facebook, Twitter, and Quora), found that startups that focus aggressively on exponential growth above all else will expedite their path to failure, exponentially.

Des Traynor, founder of Intercom, a messaging platform for websites, says that the Faustian bargain of the internet is that you can swap credibility with an audience for attention at any time. And while this "bargain" can lead to a meteoric rise in popularity for your business, your brand, or your product, it can also lead to measuring the wrong metrics (those that don't lead to profit) and, even worse, tricking customers—like accessing their address book to spamvite their friends and colleagues. This kind of growth, however exponential, at best doesn't last and at worst backfires. Metrics produced only by growth aren't always good indicators of a healthy, sustainable, profitable business, and they certainly can't compete over the long haul with customer satisfaction from an empathetic company and a well-developed product.

On the flip side of vapid and ephemeral growth-hack relationship-building is a company like Kiva, a microlending service whose entire business plan is about fostering relationships, not to grow their audience overnight but to build connections between microlenders and microloan receivers. Kiva is in the business of inserting human relationships into our financial system by helping people in impoverished countries who require a bit of money to start or run a business. People like Lindiwe, a store owner in rural Zimbabwe, tell their story on the Kiva website, providing some information about themselves, where they are from, and what they're trying to accomplish with the loan. Individuals who want to fund projects like Lindiwe's can lend a portion of the money needed, or all of it, after reading their stories.

Over time, as Lindiwe makes a profit, she repays the loan. The current rate of repayment on Kiva is 97 percent. Their network of 1.6 million lenders and 2.5 million borrowers brings together hundreds of thousands of people who would probably never meet in real life. Connecting them on the Kiva platform has generated more than $1 billion in loans so far. The magic of Kiva is that it helps build relationships and connections that lead to these microloans by showcasing the stories and lives of people who need tiny loans to build something for themselves in a place that wouldn't typically offer them loans to do so. Kiva is a relationship business whose outcome is microloans. Instead of churning and burning customer acquisition, they focus on the relationships between lenders and lendees.

A company of one finds its true north by working toward being *better,* not *bigger,* and the way to do that is to build long-term relationships with its audience and customers. Part of being better is better serving an audience who, if served well, will become customers and, if served well as customers, will become advocates. The difference between relationship companies and companies that focus solely on growth is that the former recognize that real relationships are built more slowly, in more meaningful ways, and without massive turnover. Sales aren't asked for immediately; they're brought up after relationships have developed a bit of trust. The idea is that in rewarding an audience who's giving you their attention by giving your attention back to them, through listening and empathy, you'll be rewarded with a sale (and most of the time several sales over the long term). Measuring profit or customer retention can lead to more sustainability because, as the adage goes, "What gets measured gets done." So if you're focusing on growth, growth is what will happen. But if you focus instead on *relationships* that turn into long-term customers and sales, that's what will happen instead.

How does a company of one build genuine connections in order to navigate its true north? Unfortunately, a simple desire to be authentic won't magically make us authentic, and consumers are smart enough to see our true intentions whether we want them to or not.

Chris Brogan believes that real connections are built when companies share a simple message, repeatedly, through their actions. Long before they ask for a sale, these companies articulate their message by sharing who they serve, and why. In our interview, Chris created a story on the spot that illustrates how this concept works for a business:

Imagine that your business sells fortune cookies with messages praising employees for their achievements. Your ideal customers would be HR people who are looking to reward employees for their hard work. A simple message that could be used on your website would be something along the lines of: "We're here to catch you doing something good at work." This shows the importance of praise at work and validates the product you sell (which is a good vehicle for that praise). It would make sense, as a marketing effort, to start a newsletter that showcases one great employee from your customer pool each week. This would show why praise is important and how it benefits companies that take it seriously, as well as provide an excellent example of what can be rewarded.

The newsletter isn't directly pitching your fortune cookies each week, as no one would want to subscribe to a weekly product pitch. What it does is show the potential benefits of rewarding good work, featuring your product as one specific way that can be accomplished. This message shows that, as a business first and foremost, you want your customers to succeed and thrive, and that secondarily you've got a product that can help them do that. By collecting and talking to customers constantly, you're building real personal connections with them and learning more about what they need in their business as it directly relates to what you're selling. As a company of one, your true north here is showcasing how companies can benefit from rewarding good employees — which leads to sales of fortune cookies.

BANKING SOCIAL CAPITAL

Even a company of one whose true north isn't growth requires three types of capital. The first is *financial capital,* which we learned in Chapter 11 should be as small as possible to start so that profit — achieving your MVPr — happens quickly. The second is *human capital,* which is the value that you (or your small team) bring to the business or group: this value takes the form of the skills you'll need — or your willingness to learn them — to build something and be autonomous in running it. The third type of capital required is *social capital.* While financial and human capital are important, social capital tends to be what makes or breaks a business, as it's the piece that relates to how a market or audience sees the value in what you're offering.

The term "social capital" was used intermittently as early as the beginning of the 1900s, but it gained popularity in the 1990s. Lyda Judson Hanifan is credited with coining the term in 1916; later it made a resurgence as a way to describe relationships — especially online relationships — as a form of currency. When cashed in, social capital is what you can ask people to do that benefits you (like buying your product or having someone share what you wrote with others).

The premise of social capital as the term is used today is that our social networks indeed have value. The people in those networks do things for each other, such as buying products, sharing articles, and helping each other. Relationships are currency. So companies of one need to think of social capital like a bank account. You can only take out what you put in. If you're always asking people to buy your products or doing nothing but promoting your business and its products on social media, your balance will hit zero or you may even be quickly overdrawn. People don't want to buy something from someone who is constantly bothering them on social media with "Buy my stuff!" tweets and posts or newsletters extolling the virtues of their products every week. No matter how often you ask, you won't make any sales, and no conversion tactics or growth-hacking will help.

Instead, you have to make deposits into your social capital account often and build up your balance well before you ask your audience to buy what you're selling. Do this by being helpful and creating value for as many people in your audience as possible. At the core, your social capital depends on what you can provide for your audience that educates and builds trust, value, and reputation. Social capital is built on mutually beneficial relationships, not one-sided sales-pitch-fests.

Relationships from social networks — which can be anything where people connect, not just Twitter or LinkedIn — have immense value. That's why many companies of one have mailing lists (a social network they're in control of) that drive sales. Or why many companies of one engage in conversations on social media. Relationships are the basis for building the trust required for commerce.

Buffer, our friend from previous chapters, is a company that helps people manage their social media accounts. They write daily on their blog, sharing well-written and well-researched articles about social media, which is the type of content that their audience is intensely interested in. Buffer committed to providing value, for free, right from the start and has grown to more than 1.2 million users in two years, with more than 700,000 people reading their blog each month.

Chris Guillebeau, best-selling author and creator of the World Domination Summit, personally emailed the first 10,000 people on his mailing list to thank them for signing up. Sometimes doing something that doesn't scale but is truly genuine is a great way to form strong connections with your audience. Through his authenticity and personal touch, Chris has sold more than 300,000 books and continues to sell out the WDS event each year.

There are several schools of thought about building social capital, but a popular theory put forth by Sam Milbrath of HootSuite is that you can begin by dividing your mass interactions with an audience into thirds. Sam suggests that one-third of your updates should be about your business or your content, one-third should be sharing content from others, and one-third should be personal interactions that build relationships with your audience.

Dr. Willy Bolander, assistant professor of marketing at Florida State University, and his colleague Dr. Cinthia Satornino, assistant professor of marketing at Northeastern University, found that as much as 26.6 percent of variance in sales performance comes from the social capital of a business. So building relationships by banking social capital leads directly to higher sales — sometimes as much as one-third higher. By sharing and teaching, as we've seen in previous chapters, you can establish yourself as a credible expert. And in helping people with your expertise, you can build social capital with an audience.

Social capital works because it fosters reciprocity. The more you share, provide real value and help, and connect with others, the more they'll want to help you. Danielle LaPorte, from earlier in the book, doesn't separate business relationships from her personal relationships. To her, they are the same, and she feels that all good business relationships have a strong spine of personal friendship, where both parties genuinely care about and want to help each other. These are relationships that last.

Having the empathy to learn what a consumer really wants from your company of one besides your product or service — whether it's knowledge, education, or just help — can go a long way. Empathy takes a relationship from "What can I sell you?" to "How can I truly help you?" This is the way to bank social capital: by starting a long-term and mutually beneficial relationship.

DON'T FORGET THE PEOPLE
WHO BUY FROM YOU

HighRise, a CRM (customer relationship management) company (and an offshoot business of our friends at Basecamp), does something most unusual when a person becomes a customer of their software — their support team films a personalized video for that new customer: addressing them by name, asking what help they specifically need, and giving them direct access to a human being at HighRise.

While providing these videos is definitely not a scalable system, it's an absolutely amazing relationship-builder between the business and its customers. The videos aren't professionally shot — most are taken from a shaky camera phone, with poor lighting — but they are always well received. So well received, in fact, that they tend to get shared on social media quite a bit, generating a lot of press for HighRise. Something as simple as a thirty-second video welcoming a customer to a product has real capacity to build goodwill, social capital, and genuine connection between a customer and a company.

McGill University feels so strongly that deep relationships are required with customers that they actually teach several courses and workshops on the subject. Matthew Lieberman, a professor of social cognitive neuroscience at UCLA, even goes so far as to suggest that Abraham Maslow had it quite wrong in his pyramidal hierarchy of needs when he specified physiological needs and the need for safety as humans' most basic needs. Instead, in Lieberman's estimation, belonging and connection, which Maslow defines as psychological needs, are our most basic need and should be at the bottom of the pyramid, because humans are wired to connect with each other.

Large businesses, however, in focusing on making everything quicker, often offer little real human interaction. Obviously, scalable systems are important, but only if human interaction is still at play. Too often, companies put all of their focus on turning their audience into paying customers and don't spend enough time connecting with people once they become paying customers. For Chris Brogan, and for many other companies of one, the focus stays directly on customers — by properly onboarding them, communicating with them regularly, and making sure they're getting value and use out of what he's selling. He doesn't want to make $100 off someone once; he wants to make thousands of dollars off each customer over the span of many years. This is why he focuses on customer relationships after each sale — to make sure customers are happy enough to come back again and again to buy more from him.

In their efforts to increase reach, audience, and customers, companies cannot forget about their existing customer base. Daiya Foods, a Canadian plant-based company that makes a dairy-free cheese alternative, has been popular with vegans — their core customer base — for many years. When the company was sold to the pharmaceutical giant Otsuka in the summer of 2017, its customers were outraged. By routinely testing products in animals, Otsuka, to Daiya's customers, acts in direct opposition to what vegans stand for: cruelty-free living and not harming animals. The outrage wasn't just at the consumer level either: also quickly boycotting the brand were businesses that use Daiya cheese in their commercial products — like the Toronto-based vegan pizzeria Apiecalypse Now. Going through twenty cases of Daiya per week, Apiecalypse Now placed the largest single orders for the "cheese" outside of grocery chains.

Daiya had felt that it could reach a larger customer base by selling itself to a multinational company, but the resulting sudden misalignment of values caused loyal and long-term customers to revolt. In chasing growth, Daiya ignored the main reason it had enjoyed success in the first place — by catering specifically to people who wanted to eat a plant-based diet. Petitions and boycotts quickly went up online, with thousands of ex-customers, feeling betrayed by the change in the core values on which Daiya had been founded, signing on within days of the announcement. Several retailers, like Portland's Food Fight and Brooklyn's Orchard Grocer, stopped selling Daiya immediately. Within hours, over 6,000 people signed a petition to boycott the brand.

Bear in mind that Daiya is not just an isolated incident. When Apple released its bug-filled maps software, CEO Tim Cook had to issue a public apology. When United Airlines yanked a customer from his paid-for seat, the internet exploded, and United stock plummeted by a market value of about $1 billion. When Nivea staged an ill-conceived "White Is Purity" campaign that was quickly embraced by white supremacy groups (not their target audience), the company saw a huge backlash from consumers who felt that the ad was overtly racist.

By not first considering the core group and relationship that your business serves, you can run a risk of making them feel like they don't matter — or worse, making them feel like your company doesn't care about them. At that point, they can gather their digital pitchforks and take to the streets of the internet with their outrage toward your business. And consumer outrage rarely stops at angry tweets — it causes serious business repercussions too.

Jim Dougherty, a lecturer at MIT's Sloan School of Management, has identified several key points to building relationships with customers so that they'll have an emotional and loyal stake in your business.

The first, Dougherty noted, is ensuring that customers like your business. That's a fairly obvious point, but you can't move forward in a relationship without this basic prerequisite. Going out of your way to be personal, friendly, and helpful encourages a potential customer or client to like your business more.

Second, respect must be present. Customers have to admire your work, what you offer, and how your company behaves. You build respect by doing things like following up, competently segmenting customers on your list (i.e., not pitching them products they've already purchased), and working to be the best at what you offer.

Next, customers need to admire your "whole person" — not just how you act when you're trying to sell them something. What charities do you support? How do you act outside of work? With everyone sharing everything on social media, your entire life is available to anyone with access to Google. CEOs are sharing the news when their own babies are born (like Mark Zuckerberg or Marissa Mayer). Tim Cook, an incredibly private man, shared an essay about being gay and campaigns against anti-transgender laws. Customers admire businesses that feel and act similarly to them. Admiration develops when you do this well, and once you have their admiration, customers develop an interest in your success and accomplishments instead of a sense of resentment or jealousy.

Finally, it's important that you maintain the relationship over time, even with customers who haven't financially supported your business in a while with a purchase. Consistency and longevity are key. Dougherty has found that this is where most businesses fail with relationships — that is, they drop off because they can't "find the time" when the business benefit seems to disappear. This is the exact time, however, when the relationship becomes most valuable, when a customer could be considering another purchase or heavily recommending a business to their peers or their own customers. Good relationships are the foundation to a successful business, especially for companies of one.

The return on investment from building connections with customers can manifest in several ways, like loyalty to your brand, vocal advocacy for your products, or even a reduction in churn. IBM did a study of more than 1,500 business leaders across sixty countries and thirty-three industries and found that the majority of these leaders (88 percent) viewed deeper customer relationships as the most important dimension of their business.

Building connections with customers comes down to happiness: if they're happy, they'll keep using your product or service. If they're happy, they'll tell others about your business. If they're happy, they'll stay loyal to your brand. There's no need to overthink customer relationships when the main point should always be: what can you do as a company of one to make your customers happy?

ON NOT BEING A LONE WOLF

Remember, just because you might work *for* yourself doesn't mean you have to work *by* yourself. Just as connections to an audience or paying customers are important, so too are relationships with your peers.

Angela Devlen, CEO of Wakefield Brunswick, understands the value of not being a lone wolf in business. Her company is able to do its job — consulting with large hospitals and health care facilities to help them plan for and recover from major disasters — by partnering with the top people in related fields in order to offer fuller services to its clients. These partners are not employees of Wakefield Brunswick, but they do represent her company when she brings them on for projects. It's a tight-knit and trusted network of independent business owners who work together under a single brand for a client. And conversely, if they bring her into a project, she represents their brand in the project. Each person serves on a team that is brought together for a specific project, then disbanded until they're required again. This requires no micromanaging, as these business owners are skilled at the service that's required of them, so full autonomy, with the direction of a project lead, can and does happen.

Operating this way allows Angela to run her business out of a shared coworking office (which she recommends to anyone running a small company) and to have only a single, full-time employee. This leaves the administration of her business quite light, with minimal HR obligations, and allows her greater profits from much less overhead.

Wakefield Brunswick has trusted partners only because Angela has worked hard at developing relationships with the leaders in services related to her own business. It wouldn't work for her if she hired just anyone off the street, as they wouldn't have the requisite trust to represent her brand well without first being trained extensively, which takes a lot of time.

As a company of one, Wakefield Brunswick could be limited in the size and scope of the projects it takes on, but by building connections to other independent contractors, the company can pool its expertise and skills with these other businesses and take on much bigger contracts. Remember, Wakefield Brunswick only partners with other businesses when a project requires it; otherwise, they are free to work on whatever they want. Business at every level is built on who we know and who knows us.

Similarly, Ghostly Ferns, a "family of designers," works on agency-sized projects while remaining a loose group of independent workers who all offer different design services, from illustration to branding to web application design. The team grows and shrinks as projects demand, and individual members also take on their own projects as needed. This flexibility has allowed them to work with big clients like Lincoln Motor Company, compete with and win bids from larger clients, and earn prestigious awards as well. Meg Lewis, the founder of Ghostly Ferns, believes that mixing their skills together, serving as a sounding board for each other, and generally supporting each other has led to a greater outcome than the sum of their individual skills could have achieved.

James Niehues has hand-painted more than 240 ski maps. If you've ever hit the slopes, you've probably seen his work. When Niehues was forty, he was unemployed but keenly interested in painting landscapes. So he reached out to Bill Brown, who had a monopoly on ski maps at the time, to see if he needed help. Turned out he did, and was actually about to retire. So after they did a few projects together and developed a deep connection, Brown passed all his commissions to Niehues — who has now made a living painting ski maps for thirty years.

Especially if you're working for yourself, the tendency can be to believe and then act like your company of one is in this struggle all alone and that your business needs to be just you, with no outside interaction or involvement. But in connecting with peers and fostering relationships with them, as well as with other people in our industry and even similar industries, we gain access to new ideas and a way to build valuable connections that can lead to new customers — or to simply vent. We want to retain our autonomy and independence, sure, but we also need to run with a pack from time to time, as there's strength in numbers.

BEGIN TO THINK ABOUT:

- How you could get to know your customers as real people with specific problems
- Where the true north of your business lies and what actions you could take to stay aligned with it
- How you could build relationship wealth by increasing your value and thus your social capital
- The ways in which you could empathize with your current customer base

13

■

Starting a Company
of One — My Story

S O FAR THIS BOOK HAS covered a lot of stories, data, and
studies on why growth should be questioned in the quest
to run and maintain a company of one (or really, any business you'd like to sustain long-term). Now we can move our attention to the final piece of the puzzle — what exactly we can do to go
from zero to start for a company of one.

For this chapter, we're going to focus on what it looks like to
start something on your own, even though we now know that a
company of one can flourish within a larger organization. I hope
that the material presented in this book has shown you that this
counterintuitive approach to work can benefit both your wallet
and your overall enjoyment of work, and that working for yourself can make a lot of sense. Now let's see how to put it into practice — how to build something that's too small and resilient to fail.
I'll start with my own origin story.

In the mid-1990s, I was at the University of Toronto, studying computer science and artificial intelligence — which, given
the current trends, seems like it would have been really useful to
stick with. But I hated it. I would finish studying and completing
school assignments as quickly as possible so I could focus my efforts on what I was really curious about: this new thing called the
internet, and building web pages on it with design and code.

One site I created, a dictionary for slang words (words that otherwise wouldn't be in "real" dictionaries), began to get a lot of press and notice. The attention came not just from publications that found the internet interesting and exciting, but also from design agencies that figured their clients could benefit from having websites — and they could benefit from being paid to build them.

As a result, I dropped out of school and went to work full-time at an agency in Toronto, designing and building websites. That work went well for a while, but eventually I wasn't happy with the "love 'em and leave 'em" attitude at the agency, which focused on the quantity of work more than the quality of relationships. After a year and a half of seeing that the agency wasn't keeping clients for multiple engagements, I figured the job wasn't right for me and quit to find a job at some other agency where my purpose would be more aligned with theirs.

Then a funny thing happened the day after I quit. I was all set to go to the library to figure out how to write a résumé (since I hadn't ever written one and the internet wasn't the vast resource it is now) when the phone began to ring. Clients from the agency I had just left were calling because they had heard I was no longer working there. It turns out that they had noticed my desire to deliver more value to each project and wanted to bring their business to whichever company I landed at.

I then had a thought I'd never had before — perhaps I could work for myself and build the exact type of business I wanted to run, matching my purpose with the work I was doing. Instead of going to the library to write a résumé, I went to the library to figure out how to start a business. And so began my work of almost twenty years, working for myself.

I didn't call it a company of one at the time, but in effect, that's exactly what I was doing.

In the beginning, I made far more mistakes than progress, so by telling my story, I hope I can save you a bit of heartache and the kind of real financial loss I incurred early on.

BUT FIRST, SOME CAVEATS

It seems as though every article on the internet about working for yourself extols the virtues of casting off the shackles of full-time employment to become free and happy working on your own from various beaches across the globe, with a laptop on your lap and a mai tai in your hand.

We're constantly getting the message that working for ourselves is the answer to all our problems and the only surefire way to get ahead. In fact, even though I've worked for myself longer than most people, I still don't think it's the best option for everyone. Not because some people aren't talented enough to start their own company of one, but because it just doesn't make sense for everyone. It all depends on what you want to do and how you want to do it.

When you're the boss of you, there's no HR department to handle payroll, benefits, and training. There's no accounting department to handle payables and receivables or to chase after folks who haven't paid you yet. There's no sales and marketing team drumming up new business leads for you. On top of the main skill you use to make money, you've got to do all the other jobs as well. Some folks are fine with doing this kind of work, but it may not be how others want to spend their days. The people I know with their own company of one spend approximately half of their time, or less, doing their core skill (writing, designing, programming, etc.). They spend the rest of their time on the business — chasing leads, doing their books, communicating with clients or customers, marketing, and so forth.

With all this "Work for yourself! It's better than whatever you're doing now!" messaging out there, people often end up fall-

ing in love with the idea of working for themselves without understanding the actual day-to-day work required to be their own
boss. Or as Austin Kleon cleverly puts it, *"People want to be the
noun without doing the verb."* They want the job title of founder or
CEO, or a business card and a fancy website with a new logo, but
they forget or overlook the daily rigors of running a business of
their own. Having a brilliant idea or a passion to build a successful business is not enough. Ideas and dreams are nice, but they're
also cheap and meaningless if you don't take action and do the
work to make them happen.

The harder—much harder—part is making the dream happen every day. Some days you're buried in accounting spread-
sheets; other days, you're on the third round of revisions from a
client, or dealing with an irate customer. The daily slog is what
separates wannabe business owners from those who make it a
reality.

Working for yourself requires ego and purpose in equal measure. I started working for myself because I figured I could foster
client relationships better than the agency where I worked. That
became my purpose—not to be the best designer (which I'm not
even sure is possible), but to run a business focused on client relationships. So ego is involved, not in a bad way but in a "I know
I can do this better" sort of way. If you don't think it's possible to
do better, or you don't care if it is, there's no point doing your own
thing. In that case, it's fine to work for someone else—they're already established and have people handling the jobs you probably
don't want to be doing anyway.

Purpose is required in that you have to have a north star that
will drive you long-term without blinking out. A desire to get rich
quick or achieve business fame isn't going to motivate you for
long, since neither is quickly possible, regardless of who you are.
There are much easier ways to make money or become famous in
the world. Why do you want to work for yourself? What will drive

you to keep going when things get rough or take longer than you hoped they would? What will make it worth it when you're stuck in the day-to-day minutiae of running a business?

For myself, I happen to like choices. I like that I can choose to make less money by saying no to a project or a client or a customer I don't think is a good fit for me. I like that I can choose to unplug for three months at a time and go on camping road trips across American deserts with my wife. I like that I can pick what I work on next, rather than have work handed down to me. I like that I can work on Saturday if I want, and go hiking on Wednesday. This freedom of choice is my north star. Yes, it's taken some time to get here, and I had to be okay with not having nearly as much freedom in the beginning as I do now. After all, bills need to be paid and sometimes the best client isn't the best fit but he's the one who's here right now and willing to pay you this month. Still, even in the rough patches, my purpose — my freedom of choice — is what's driven me forward.

I don't mean to give you a downer of a message — only to challenge your idea of wanting to work for yourself, just as you should challenge the notion that all growth is beneficial. If you're like "Yes, I'm in," then that's awesome — I hope this book gives you a bit of a roadmap to building your own company of one. But if it doesn't make sense for you right now (or ever), that's okay too. Perhaps your path is becoming a company of one at the organization you're part of and building a brilliant and resilient career there. I would never say that there's one singular path to business success and enjoyment for everyone to take.

THE BUILD

Let's say I had to start my business tomorrow from scratch, with no existing clients or following. How would I build an audience? How would I attract customers?

This is how lots of people start businesses every day: knowing how to do something well (their craft), but without an existing group of people eager to work with them. Where do you begin?

With my skill set, I'd start by listening to people who are looking to hire web designers or have already hired web designers, since that's the most marketable skill I've got. How are these potential clients conducting their search for a designer? Where are they searching? What questions do they have about the process? If they've had a bad experience with a web designer, what went wrong? What do they wish they'd known before starting a web design project?

Then I'd offer to help with their questions. Is there anything in particular they want to know? Do they want a second set of eyes to look at something? Do they want to brainstorm on what to do next? Do they want a second opinion? Is there anything they want to know about the industry? I would add small bits of helpful advice without offering my own services or charging them. More important, I wouldn't be pushy about it — I'd just look for folks who have questions I have answers to.

This free help I offer wouldn't be a month of work or a redesign of their whole website, but rather emails and chats, either in person or by phone or Skype. Basically, I would offer a free consult or a project roadmapping session. In this way, I'd learn the key factors involved when people are thinking about hiring a web designer and gain insight into why and how they end up choosing to hire one.

Just like Alex Franzen in Chapter 4, I'd start by finding a single person to offer my knowledge to. Then another. And another. I'd talk to as many people as possible, until I start to notice definite trends where people are having issues or not understanding things. And I'd do all of this without pitching or selling myself once. I'd simply offer help or advice to anyone who wants it.

Talking to people this way would do two things. First, it gives me be an opportunity to share my knowledge with the type of people I want to work with (without asking for anything in return). Second, I'd learn what my future audience is looking for, where they're getting hung up in projects in my field, and how I can communicate with them effectively to help solve those problems.

Long before I'd start selling anyone anything, I'd be building relationships with the people I've helped in some way. I wouldn't build this following so I could "promote" or sell to them later. I'd build and foster relationships with these people so I could continue learning from them. And these would be mutually beneficial relationships: they'd receive my help and I'd receive their knowledge.

Most important, I'd do this fact-finding/mini-consulting while I was working somewhere else, probably at a full-time job. I wouldn't dive headfirst into building my own company from the ground up, because I wouldn't know yet if it was an idea that I could execute well enough to make into a sustainable living.

From there the path could go several ways. Through a blog, I could write publicly about what I learned and eventually compile my posts into a book — full of insight into common client issues and how they can be resolved (as I did in writing a previous book). Or I could use my newly acquired knowledge to create my own services, since I'd know where my potential audience needed the most help. I'd probably do both things, with confidence that the people I'd been helping would promote what I came up with, and with no need on my part to constantly promote/sell at them.

And this is the key — the people I'd helped would help me precisely because I had helped them (although I would never expect it of them). In my own company of one, every single business I consulted with or roadmapped for wanted to hire me to execute the plan I'd helped them come up with. Even when I was charging good money for consulting, I'd still be at the top of each client's list to hire. Being helpful proved to be a great lead-generation funnel.

My new business would be based on helping others first, with a contract for web design or design consulting coming later. I'd do it this way not because I frown on capitalism and want to sit around a Skype video-call singing "Kumbaya," but because I know this is how you build a loyal client base and following.

Many people would view this approach as advice for building a charity or aiming a business only at your close friends — it couldn't possibly be applied to a business that makes enough money to put clothes on the children, keep food on the table, and pay the rent. But this is precisely how I built a business that, for over a decade, has had a waiting list of four to five months. It's how I released books that have sold tens of thousands of copies. It's how I've approached my entrepreneurial work for years. I've simply used my skills to help others, because I enjoy doing it. And I've offered this help for free, in small doses at first, and then later for good money in larger doses.

This approach mirrors the mind-set of a company of one, in that you can start right away, without investing a ton of money in resources, tools, or automation software. You can hit your MVPr quickly by offering services first, then products as demand increases for those services. To get started, you need a computer and an internet connection, and that's it.

The best thing about gearing your business to make money now rather than spending money now to maybe make more money later is that profit happens faster. You don't need investors, or investment on your part, or investments from venture capitalists. There's no need for a certain hardware or software, and no need to use secret tactics or strategies. All you need is to be a decent human being with a valued skill set and a willingness to share what you know with people who'll listen.

My own company started this way, after I decided not to find another agency job. At the time I was still a teenager, living at home and working in my parents' basement on a computer I had built myself out of cheap parts. I focused on the work I could do immediately in order to make enough money to cover living expenses once I moved out (which I did quickly, heading west) and then to not only make a living but save as much as I could.

The traditional way to establish a business is to start by getting an investment (from the bank, from a rich relative, from a VC), then work hard for a long time to create a perfect product. This way of working, however, has a lot of drawbacks. You have to make a ton of assumptions about the market, your positioning, and your customers, and then, before launching, you have to spend a lot of money and then just wait for the results to come in.

Taking the opposite approach, the company-of-one approach, can work just as well, if not better. Being able to launch your business without any investment (other than a tiny bit of your own time), you don't have to make as many assumptions about the market, your product, or your potential customers. You can start your company of one simply by making your business idea as small as possible, then launching quickly.

For example, Creative Class (my own first online course) started out as an idea for thirty lessons, which would have taken me four to six months to create. I also wanted to develop course software to run it (another four to six months of work). I resisted the urge to spend four to six months writing lessons, however, and instead started with seven lessons and existing software; this way I could launch in a month instead of a year. The quick launch enabled me to see what worked and what didn't with an actual audience, and then I could adjust, iterate, and improve. After starting with seven lessons, I added seven more, based on the feedback I received from students. With the second round of seven lessons, I was able to get my course out quickly, have it generate money, and then adjust it based on real feedback from paying customers. By the sixth version of the course, it was making enough money to sustain me.

THE SETUP

While obviously the company-of-one method is to start with as little as possible and then grow it slowly or as needed, there are still some factors that need to be considered.

Money

Too often businesses focus only on revenue. For companies of one, expenses are just as important, since the sooner you can reach MVPr the better.

Let's look at it this way. If you offer a service for $1,000 and your monthly expenses are $2,000, then you need at least three clients per month to be profitable. If you need $4,000 to cover your expenses, then you need at least five clients to be profitable. Honestly consider two questions: In the beginning, can you reduce any of your expenses so that you can do less work to be profitable each month? And how likely is it that you'll get the number of clients or customers you need each month to be profitable? If acquiring three clients seems doable but having five would stretch you too thin, you've got to either reduce your overall costs or raise your rates. Consider how long it takes to find a client, court the client, work with the client, and then finish up each client's project. Is there enough time in a month to do that five times? Or even three?

The same questions need to be asked of a product business. If you price your product at $50 and your costs are $30, then you don't need to sell 40 products ($2,000/$50 gross = 40 units) to reach $2,000; rather, you need to sell 100 ($2,000/$20 in profit = 100 units). Again, if your expenses are $4,000, you need to sell 200 units. How likely is that?

Another factor related to money is how you spend your time. Every day you spend developing a product is a day you aren't really making money from it, unless you've done preorders or crowdfunding. How can you get an initial version of your product to market quickly to start building revenue?

Money is why a lot of companies of one begin as side projects: their path to MVPr in order to cover the founder's expenses can take a bit of time. I offset my own living expenses at first by living at home with my parents (hey, I was only nineteen), and then by taking a few years to slowly transition fully from services to products — and not until the products were routinely making more than what I was charging for services.

Legal

Small businesses can be taken advantage of, ripped off, or screwed out of money they're owed — sometimes by larger businesses, but sometimes by businesses the same size. This is why having legal systems in place right from the start is important.

You need to ensure, first, that your business entity is set up properly for the country and region you're operating from, and second, that your business is removed by one layer from you personally. In other words, your business should be its own legal entity — a corporation in most countries or an LLC in the United States. That way, should anything go wrong in your business, it is your business that is liable, not you personally. All money should go into your business directly, not straight to you, and then you should be paid out, by salary or dividends. There are so many different ways to structure a business — based on your needs, what you provide to clients or customers, and where you're located — that you probably need a lawyer (and an accountant sometimes) to help you set up the right business for you.

Next, after you've separated your company of one from yourself personally, you need to prevent your company from being taken advantage of. With service-based businesses, this means having contracts between your business and your clients. In the beginning, you can source contracts fairly cheaply online. Eventually, it makes sense to enlist the help of a lawyer who's familiar with both your area of practice and how laws work in your geographic location and who, of course, can make sure that your contract is sound. For a product-based business, this means having users agree to your terms of service before they pay you for what you're selling.

The reason for having a business lawyer — and one who's on contract, not an employee — is not so that you can sue everyone, but so that lawsuits rarely happen. I pay my own business lawyer a small yearly fee as a retainer so that I can ask him a few questions now and then, as a preventive measure. He makes sure not only that the threat of my business being sued is as small as possible, but that the need for my business to sue anyone else is as small as possible too. Having to take someone to court, or being taken to court, would put a lot of stress and strain on the daily operations of my company of one.

The best lawyer for a company of one is one who understands the type of business you do and is happy to work with a business of your size. And in general, I've found out the hard way that it's never a smart idea to be either the biggest or the smallest client of anyone you hire for their professional services.

Accounting

I've always believed that good accountants should save you more money than they charge. This belief may be misguided — I have no studies or data to back it up — but nevertheless, my own accountants definitely do this.

To find the best accountant for your company of one, look for a firm or individual who has knowledge of your type of work and familiarity with businesses of your size. My own business needs a firm that understands how online business works, and how to deal with revenue that comes from selling digital products primarily in the United States (in U.S. dollars) while my business is in Canada (operating in Canadian dollars).

An accountant is not just a person you talk to at the end of your business year when you file your taxes. You can use an accountant as an adviser on all things related to government requests, on how to stay up to date with financial laws (so you don't inadvertently break them), on sound ways to pay yourself and pay your expenses, and on how best to structure your business to pay the least amount in taxes.

I talk to my own accountant every few months — whenever I'm thinking about making any changes, adding a new product or partnership, or anticipating a new and large expense — or anytime I get a letter from the government to my business (since those typically aren't written in understandable language). I also have my accountant audit my bookkeeping to ensure that everything is done correctly and nothing is missed. I would rather focus on making money than have to figure out the convoluted details of how much I owe the government, so I gladly lean on my accountant for this service. Again, I hire accountants as independent consultants, not as employees, as a company of one doesn't need a full-time accountant.

Salary

As I mentioned in the legal section, you need to make sure your business is separated from yourself, and to this end, the first thing you need to do is open a separate bank account for your business and then, from that account, pay yourself either a dividend or a salary. Since revenue from my work can sometimes be inconsistent, I've always figured my base salary as the average I've made in profit (not revenue) for the last twelve months, minus 25 to 30 percent (to set aside for taxes). Before raising my salary if my profits increase, I also take into consideration the minimum amount I need each month to live on and be comfortable. With my twelve-month average profit in mind, and not going too far past my minimum living expenses, I can set myself a fairly steady salary. Obviously, you can change this up if you find you need less money — or more — but keep in mind that the more money you take out of your business, the more it's taxed.

The biggest thing to consider when you work for yourself is that even if you're paying yourself the average of the last twelve months, there's no guarantee you'll make the same profit moving forward. That's why it's important to have a "runway buffer" — a bit of savings to cover yourself and your expenses if there's a slow month or two. Because I like to play it very safe, I have a six-month runway buffer of liquid assets that I can easily and quickly access if I need to. Other people I know are comfortable with a three-month buffer, so just decide yourself what works for you. Personally, I wasn't even willing to start working on my own full-time until I had a runway buffer saved up.

Another factor in how much you pay yourself is how much time off you'd like. If you want to take four weeks a year as vacation, then you'll need to set aside a month's worth of extra savings (on top of your runway buffer). Unless you've got a recurring income stream (like recurring revenue from monthly software licenses), if you aren't working, you may not be making money.

Having a runway buffer of liquid savings also helps when unexpected events come up. A family member falling ill or passing away can require you to take time off that you hadn't planned for. In this event a recurring income stream and runway buffer can be a great help at a difficult time.

Savings

Alongside a salary and a runway buffer, I truly think companies of one should invest as much money as they can save up in passive investments like index funds. If inflation is approximately 3 percent per year, then you're losing money on any assets you've got that aren't making at least 3 percent per year in returns. This applies, by the way, to all the money in your bank account, since checking and savings accounts pay barely any interest.

Since I don't have an employer putting money into a 401(k) or Registered Retirement Savings Plan, created by the Canadian government for Canadians like me, I've got to consider how I can make the most of being in the prime of my earning potential and save for the future, when that might not be the case. And just as I do with my salary, I have an automatic withdrawal set up to transfer money from my bank account into my investment account each month—in an amount that's high enough to matter long-term but low enough not to affect my liquid assets.

The goal here is to work your money in small steps. First, ensure that your company of one is making enough profit to cover your living expenses. Second, make sure you've got enough of a runway buffer built up to work full-time at your company of one, even if things get slow. Third, with your salary and runway buffer covered, you can reinvest money in your company; if things are going well, you should be able to get a better than 3 percent return on such an investment. Alternatively, if you don't need to invest more in your company—maybe your business costs are covered and you have no reason to grow them—you can invest any extra money in something like index funds.

I use a robo-investor with very low management fees and keep my money in index funds that require no upkeep on my end. Once a quarter, I check in on my investments, and if I have questions I talk to someone at the company. But since these investments are long-term, I'm not worried about daily or even monthly losses or gains. I just want to see my money grow over decades.

Health Coverage

Depending on the country you live in, medical coverage and insurance can be a huge factor in deciding if you're going to go on your own and start a company of one.

Jonnie Hallman, the founder of Cushion (which offers scheduling software for freelancers), found that the number-one reason his fellow Americans don't venture out and start their own companies is their worry about the cost of health care. Insurance can definitely cost more when you aren't part of an employer or group plan, so shop around before you make your choice.

Luckily in many other countries, like Canada, basic health care is available to every citizen. Canadians only have to worry about obtaining extended medical insurance, critical injury insurance (in case they're injured for a long period of time), and life insurance. But in the United States, health care coverage continues to be an issue. As a company of one, you'll definitely find it worth your while to do some outreach to see where you can obtain health and life insurance.

Regardless of where you're located, there are usually groups you can join to take advantage of bulk savings, such as professional associations, chambers of commerce, and business groups.

Lifestyle

And now, with the nitty-gritty of money and insurance coverage out of the way, we can turn to the question of the lifestyle you want your company of one to allow you to have. Regardless of the type of work you do, how you work is always going to involve a lifestyle choice. The benefit of a company of one is that you can build your lifestyle around it, optimizing for both profit and your own happiness.

The first step is to develop a consistent, healthy monthly revenue to cover costs, your runway buffer, and investments. Once you take care of those considerations, a beautiful thing happens: you're presented with choices. You can choose to make more money, if that's what you want, or you can choose to work the same and make the same amount. If you make the latter choice, you can then start to prioritize. Do you want to spend more time with your family? Do you want to explore the world? Do you want to spend more time experimenting with new business ideas and opportunities?

By removing the hurdle of having to consider scaling up in all areas at all times when things are going well, you can open yourself up to investing in enjoying your own life. You will have the freedom to enjoy the benefits of having figured out how to make "enough."

And then, if our goals are similar, I hope to see you out hiking on the trails in the wild Pacific Northwest one day soon.

BEGIN TO THINK ABOUT:

- Your purpose or reasoning in starting your own company of one, and whether it will hold up over time
- How you could start your own company of one right now, with some first version of what you want to do
- What you need to do to set up your company of one correctly and responsibly, both legally and financially

Afterword:
Never Grow Up

There's a hotel nestled in the picturesque countryside of Japan's Yamanashi prefecture, the Nishiyama Onsen Keiunkan, which is the oldest continuously run hotel in the world. It has been in existence for about 1,300 years (it opened its doors in AD 705) and managed by fifty-two generations of the same family.

Empires have risen and fallen around Onsen Keiunkan, great wars have ravaged it, and massive economic booms and busts have come and gone. Still, the hotel has endured and remained profitable enough to stay open for business. The hotel has thirty-five rooms and access to six natural hot spring baths, which are open 24/7 to better serve their guests. The water of the baths is pure, alkaline, and neither artificially heated nor treated. The hotel serves simple, seasonal food, locally sourced from the surrounding mountains and rivers. Besides the baths, there are no other attractions in the nearby area, and there's definitely no wifi or ride-sharing. Still, it's been a popular destination for far longer than any of us (or our great-grandparents) have been alive. Guests have included emperors, politicians, samurai, and military commanders.

The hotel's focus, since the beginning, has been on customer service, *not on* growth or expansion. It's stayed small because the top priority has always been making guests comfortable.

How the Onsen Keiunkan has succeeded by not choosing exponential growth is a story best told by looking at its peer: the oldest continuously run business in the world, Kongō Gumi, a Buddhist temple construction company. The founder, Kongo Shigemitsu, saw an incredible opportunity: Buddhism was catching on quickly, and so temples needed to be built. For the next fourteen centuries (i.e., long after the founder's death), the company kept busy building temples. Like their hotel peer, Kongō Gumi kept a relentless focus on serving customers and being absolute experts at their craft, and that focus enabled the construction company to be resilient enough to endure.

For 1,428 years, Kongō Gumi hummed along as a construction company. Things suddenly changed, however, when they decided to expand into real estate during a boom in the Japanese market in the 1980s due to an epic financial bubble and unconstrained credit growth. For a while, Kongō Gumi reaped the short-term rewards of fast growth, but as so often happens, that growth wasn't sustainable.

By the start of the 1990s, the financial bubble had completely burst in Japan. Companies that took on vast amounts of borrowed money with artificially suppressed interest rates were left with nothing but debt. Debt was like a popular drug — everyone was doing it and every business seemed to have access to it.

Kongō Gumi ended up with close to $343 million in debt. It was sold to a larger company and ultimately liquidated a few years later — bringing its extremely long run as a company to an end. The temple construction company had survived countless political crises, two atomic detonations, and even a period when the Japanese government set out to eradicate Buddhism from Japan completely. But ironically, what they couldn't survive was the cost of rapid growth. Their downfall was putting growth above stability and profit.

In Japanese, *shinise* is the word for a long-lasting company. Interestingly, about 90 percent of all businesses worldwide that are more than 100 years old are Japanese. They all have fewer than 300 employees, and the ones that still exist never grow quickly or without great reason.

Onsen Keiunkan, by contrast, has barely grown at all. Still operating with fewer than forty rooms and six hot springs, they've survived by recognizing that growth isn't required for long-term success. Making every customer feel like they are the one and only customer, the hotel has been dedicated to service in a way that has drawn intergenerational patronage (which isn't something many companies ever see). They have done some updating, of course, redoing the rooms in the 1990s and digging a new well, but these iterations have been slight and carefully thought out.

Onsen Keiunkan has survived, not in spite of being small, but because of it. They didn't expand into a hotel chain, or turn their interests to real estate investing, or follow the whims of market booms. They haven't taken on investors or gone public.

To put this all into perspective, Richard Foster, a lecturer at the Yale School of Management, found that the average life span of a business on the S&P 500 is only fifteen years total.

Onsen Keiunkan, on the other hand, has been in business and operating for 1,300 years.

BECOMING TOO SMALL TO FAIL

The ideas, research cited, and lessons in this book point to a broader philosophy of business achievement: business success does not lie in growing something quickly and massively, but rather in building something that's both remarkable and resilient over the long term. This isn't to say that success happens only after the first millennium has passed, but that success is about finding a way to sustain a business as long as it needs to be sustained. As we've seen time and time again, nothing is too big to fail. With bigger scale come bigger dangers, bigger risks, and much work to become and remain profitable.

Instead, you can focus on building something that, in effect, is too small to fail. You can adapt a small company of one to ride out recessions, adjust to changing customer motivations, and ignore competition by being smaller, more focused, and in need of much less to turn a profit.

Success, then, ought not to be measured by quarterly profit increases or ever-growing customer acquisition, or even by your ability to create an exit strategy and leave with more than you entered with. Instead, as Natasha Lampard of the popular internet conference "WebStock" says, you can focus on an "exist strategy" — based on sticking around, profiting, and serving your customers as best you can. Your success can be measured by being profitable quickly as you stay small and build real relationships with your customers — not because you're an altruistic hippie, but because it pays off over time. Long-term, loyal customers will sometimes hang around for generations, continuing to financially support your business.

A better problem to solve — one that requires real ingenuity — is how to avoid dealing with everything that comes up by just adding more to the mix. Solving business problems by simply adding more is like putting a Band-Aid on a cut — yes, it might stop the bleeding, but covering it up doesn't help you deal with why the cut happened in the first place. To add more is basically an effort to fix an existing problem without first looking at its cause.

If you figure out why you need more, you can come to better conclusions, ones that might actually help both your business and your customers. Maybe you can turn down growth that doesn't serve your company. Maybe you can create and sustain a tiny business that doesn't overwork you or your staff and doesn't ignore customers and still profits wildly. Maybe instead of taking investments to grow, you can remain the same size.

Instead of solving problems with more, perhaps you can determine what is basically enough. Ricardo Semler, whom I quoted at the start of this book, believes that profit past the minimum isn't essential for business survival. He likens going for profit at all costs to seeing a jail with empty cells and assuming that not enough prisoners have been rounded up yet. In effect, what's best for the government that runs the jail isn't a spike in the crime rate so that more people can be punished, but a greater effort to make sure crime doesn't happen in the first place, thereby creating more taxpayers and more profit for them.

My mind keeps coming back to the two studies showing that growth is the main cause of failure in so many startups, and even many top corporations. The truth is, very few startups last for a long time. Most of them don't even last a few years let alone fifteen years, and certainly not 1,300 years. When they grew, many of them simply became too big to succeed. Big companies can find it so much easier to fail, with their higher burn rates, the rampant acquisition they require to hit profitable status, and their huge teams full of people you hope are pulling their own weight, but who knows? There are too many people on them to know for certain.

Determining what is enough is different for everyone. Enough is the antithesis of growth. Enough is the true north of building a company of one, and the opposite of the current paradigm promoting entrepreneurship, growth-hacking, and a startup culture.

Growth, as we've seen from the studies and stories presented in this book, is not an unalterable law of business. Instead, growth doesn't have to inevitably follow success or profit, especially for a company of one. When you become too small to fail, you also become small enough to make your own choices about your work. Real freedom is gained when you define upper bounds to your goals and figure out what your own personal sense of enough is. You'll have the freedom to say no to doing the expected, or to opportunities that don't serve you.

There's a satisfaction in reaching the point of enough in your business, and then knowing that you don't have to explore every new potential opportunity that comes up. This freedom allows you to run your company of one in your own way — a way that gives you a life you enjoy, fills your days with tasks you actually want to do, and brings you customers you actually want to serve.

THIS IS JUST THE BEGINNING

This book has been an exploration of the concept of a "company of one" by looking at research and examples of people who have asked, "What if . . .?" What if growth doesn't matter? What happens when we put an upper bound on our goals? What if business and capitalism itself are turned on their head?

As I started out on this journey to explore companies of one, I figured I was alone in my belief that growth isn't always the best course of action for business. But then, as I explored the idea more, I realized that a silent movement is happening. Companies of one around the world are starting to succeed, making substantial profits, without rapidly hiring employees or taking venture capital. Companies like Buffer and Basecamp are thriving and profitable, and people like Tom Fishburne and Danielle LaPorte are challenging the status quo and building smaller but amazing businesses.

Remember that technically everyone is a company of one — or at least, they should be. Even if you lead a team at a business that isn't yours, or you are an employee at a massive company, no one else truly cares as much about your career as you do. Indeed, it's your sole responsibility to look out for your own interests, and it's up to you to define and then achieve whatever success means to you.

Most of us know that the perception that being an entrepreneur is riskier than being a corporate worker is misguided, since at a large corporation these days employees have little control as to how it's run, how it focuses on profit (or on growth), and how secure their jobs really are. Yes, starting something on your own can be a little risky too, but I've found that most entrepreneurs are the most risk-averse people I know. They iterate on ideas and move slowly when it comes to risk, but move quickly to create profit (since they need profit in order to pay themselves).

By becoming a company of one, or just by adopting the key aspects of this mind-set, you can develop the resilience required to thrive in any job, at any company, or with any project or business you start on your own. By making sure your business works when it's as small as possible, you can ensure that it will work if and when it grows.

There's a point — and it's different for everyone — where you realize that having more won't affect your quality of life. When your "enough" happens, it should be liberating. What's the difference, really, between having $90 million and having $900 million? (Honestly, I wouldn't know.) If you're not sure you've reached that point, question why you want more, or why what you have isn't enough.

Accepting the mind-set of a company of one doesn't have to be an either-or decision. Don't feel that you have to take it or leave it. Instead, I challenge you to consider how specific ingredients in the overall recipe put forward in this book could benefit the way you work or the way your business operates. Perhaps you can adopt some ideas and leave the rest. As long as you're questioning concepts and determining what's best for your own business and customers, I'll be happy.

Today more than ever, behemoth corporations need to learn how to be more nimble and maverick, more like a company of one. And people who are just starting down their own path, toward their own business, need to know that there's another path forward. In fact, there are infinite paths, and unless you start asking questions about each pathway, you may not enjoy where you end up.

Everything in this book derives from my belief that all companies, of every size, should be "lifestyle" businesses, not trapped in the paradigm of how "real" businesses operate. In fact, every business, theoretically, is a lifestyle business, in that each represents your choice of how you want to live. If you want to work in the fast-paced corporate world, you have to accept that your life will have little room for much else. If you choose the growth-focused venture capital world, you have to accept being beholden to two groups of people: investors and customers (and what each wants could be vastly different). And if you work in a company where *enough* profit is acceptable, then your lifestyle can be optimized for more than just growing profit.

In sum, all business is a choice about the life we want outside of it. One choice isn't better than any other; all are simply choices, guided by our own internal and deeply personal factors. This book presents one choice. It may not be the choice you'd make on how to run your life and your business, but if it is, I hope that this book has given you both a bit of insight and a small light to guide you.

There's *only* one rule for being a company of one: stay attentive to those opportunities that require growth and question them before taking them. That's it — one rule. The rest is entirely up to you. But if you ever stop questioning the need for growth, you run the risk that the beast of growth will devour you and your business whole.

The company-of-one movement is constantly growing (bad joke, I couldn't help myself). If you've got a company-of-one story of your own to share, I'd love to hear it (paul@mightysmall.co). I read every email and reply to as many as I can — I promise.

The more products, the more markets, the more alliances a company makes, the less money it makes. "Full speed ahead in all directions" seems to be the call from the corporate bridge. When will companies learn that line extension ultimately leads to oblivion.

— AL RIES AND JACK TROUT,
The 22 Immutable Laws of Marketing

Acknowledgments

Books are team efforts in which one person (the author) gets to take all the credit. So, my thanks go out to all the people whose names wouldn't fit on the cover with mine:

To my wife, Lisa, who's always willing to encourage me when that's needed, and to kick me in the ass when that's needed as well.

To my amazing agent, Lucinda Blumenfeld, my equally amazing editor, Rick Wolff, his wonderful assistant Rosemary McGuinness, and everyone else at Lucinda Literary and Houghton Mifflin Harcourt. You've all lifted this book to a level far beyond what I could have dreamed of or reached on my own.

To the folks who let me interview them for this book. I was totally hitting above my weight with my interview requests, but lucked out when these people agreed to talk and share with me: Chris Brogan, Kate O'Neill, Katie Womserley, Marshall Haas, Miranda Hixon, Tom Fishburne, Alex Beauchamp, Angela Devlen, Brian Clark, Danielle LaPorte, Glen Urban, James Clear, Jason Fried, Jeff Sheldon, Jessica Abel, Sean D'Souza, Jocelyn Glei, Kyle Murphy, Kaitlin Maud, Rand Fishkin, Sol Orwell, Zach McCullough, and everyone else I spoke with in writing this book.

To my "rat people," my longtime readers who let me email them every Sunday morning with whatever wacky and mostly counterintuitive idea I want to share on my newsletter. Thanks for reading, for sharing, and for encouraging. Without you all, none of this would be possible.

To you, for reading this book. I hope what I've shared can inspire or cast a different light on your work.

Notes

PROLOGUE

page

xii *people would rather get electric shocks:* Timothy D. Wilson, David A. Reinhard, Erin C. Westgate, Daniel T. Gilbert, Nicole Ellerbeck, Cheryl Hahn, Casey L. Brown, and Adi Shaked, "Just Think: The Challenges of the Disengaged Mind," *Science* 345, no. 6192 (July 4, 2014): 75–77.

1. DEFINING A COMPANY OF ONE

7 *The word "intrapreneur":* Gifford Pinchot III, "Who Is the Intrapreneur?" in *Intrapreneuring: Why You Don't Have to Leave the Corporation to Become an Entrepreneur* (New York: HarperCollins, 1985), 28–48.

8 *In a recent study:* Vijay Govindarajan and Jatin Desai, "Recognize Intrapreneurs Before They Leave," *Harvard Business Review* (September 20, 2013), http://www.meritaspartners.com/wp-content/uploads/2013/12/Recognize-Intrapreneurs-Before-They-Leave.pdf.

12 *42 percent of jobs are at risk:* Creig Lamb, "The Talented Mr. Robot: The Impact of Automation on Canada's Workforce," Brookfield Institute for Innovation + Entrepreneurship, Toronto, June 2016, http://brookfieldinstitute.ca/research-analysis/automation/, 3–8.

within the next ten to twenty years: Council of Economic Advisers, *Economic Report to the President: Together with the Annual Report of the Council of Economic Advisers* (Washington, D.C.: White House, February 2016), https://obamawhitehouse.archives.gov/sites/default/files/docs/ERP_2016_Book_Complete%20JA.pdf.

15 *employee satisfaction goes up, and turnover goes down:* Cali Ressler and Jody Thompson, *Why Work Sucks and How to Fix It* (New York: Portfolio, 2010), 11–36.

16 *more than one-third of jobs in America:* Edelman Intelligence, *Freelancing in America 2016*, commissioned by Upwork and Freelancers Union, October 6, 2016, https://www.slideshare.net/upwork/freelancing-in-america-2016/1.

2. STAYING SMALL AS AN END GOAL

27 *74 percent of those businesses failed:* Max Marmer, Bjoern Lasse Herrmann, Ertan Dogrultan, and Ron Berman, "Startup Genome Report Extra on Premature Scaling," Startup Genome, San Francisco, CA, August

29, 2011, http://innovationfootprints.com/wp-content/uploads/2015/07/startup-genome-report-extra-on-premature-scaling.pdf.

27 *the Kauffman Foundation and Inc. magazine did a follow-up study*: Jason Wiens and Chris Jackson, "The Importance of Young Firms for Economic Growth," Ewing Marion Kauffman Foundation, Kansas City, MO, September 2015, http://www.kauffman.org/what-we-do/resources/entrepreneurship-policy-digest/the-importance-of-young-firms-for-economic-growth.

30 *left the company*: Joel Gascoigne, "Change at Buffer: The Next Phase, and Why Our Co-Founder and Our CTO Are Moving On," *Buffer Open*, February 10, 2017, https://open.buffer.com/change-at-buffer/.

35 *earns $400,000 a year*: Pieter Levels, interview by Courtland Allen, Indie Hackers, July 2016, https://www.indiehackers.com/businesses/nomad-list.

39 *the number of non-employee establishments*: U.S. Census data cited in Elaine Pofeldt, "How to Find Your Million-Dollar, One-Person Business Idea," *Forbes*, May 27, 2017, https://www.forbes.com/sites/elainepofeldt/2017/05/27/how-to-find-your-million-dollar-business-idea-by-tapping-new-census-data/#3ac375a343d9.

3. WHAT'S REQUIRED TO LEAD

46 *Research from the University of Lausanne business school*: John Antonakis, Marika Fenley, and Sue Liechti, "Can Charisma Be Taught? Tests of Two Interventions," Academy of Management: Learning and Education 10, no. 3 (2011): 374–396.

47 *found that introverted leaders*: Adam Grant, Francesca Gino, and David A. Hofmann, "The Hidden Advantages of Quiet Bosses," *Harvard Business Review* (December 2010), https://hbr.org/2010/12/the-hidden-advantages-of-quiet-bosses.

49 *empowered, self-directed, or autonomous teams*: Drita Kruja, Huong Ha, Elvisa Drishti, and Ted Oelfke, "Empowerment in the Hospitality Industry in the United States," *Journal of Hospitality Marketing and Management* (March 3, 2015).

52 *"a little bit about a lot"*: Meghan Casserly, "The Secret Power of the Generalist — And How They'll Rule the Future," *Forbes*, July 10, 2010, https://www.forbes.com/sites/meghancasserly/2012/07/10/the-secret-power-of-the-generalist-and-how-theyll-rule-the-future/#57821b312bd5.

55 *stop hustling*: David Heinemeier Hansson, "Trickle-down Workaholism in Startups," *Signal vs. Noise,* May 30, 2017, https://m.signalvnoise.com/trickle-down-workaholism-in-startups-a90ceac76426.

Workaholism: Wayne E. Oates, *Confessions of a Workaholic: The Facts About Work Addiction* (Nashville, TN: Abingdon Press, 1971).

56 *the term "power paradox":* Jerry Useem, "Power Causes Brain Damage," *Atlantic,* July/August 2017, https://www.theatlantic.com/magazine /archive/2017/07/power-causes-brain-damage/528711/.
qualities that lead to the leadership roles: Useem, "Power Causes Brain Damage."

58 *when people take the time:* Rik Kirkland interview with Adam Grant, "Wharton's Adam Grant on the Key to Professional Success," McKinsey & Company, June 2014, https://www.mckinsey.com/business-functions /organization/our-insights/whartons-adam-grant-on-the-key-to -professional-success.

4. GROWING A COMPANY THAT DOESN'T GROW

63 *five times as much as keeping an existing one:* Graham Charlton, "Companies More Focused on Acquisition Than Retention: Stats," *Econsultancy,* New York, August 30, 2015, https://econsultancy.com/blog/63321 -companies-more-focused-on-acquisition-than-retention-stats.
finding new customers: "Cross-Channel Marketing Report 2013," *Econsultancy,* New York, August 2013, https://econsultancy.com/reports/cross -channel-marketing-report-2013.

64 "You can't sell your way": Gary Sutton, *Corporate Canaries: Avoid Business Disasters with a Coal Miner's Secrets* (Nashville, TN: Thomas Nelson, Inc., 2005).
Steve Martin has had similar thoughts: Steve Martin, "Steve Martin Teaches Comedy," MasterClass, https://www.masterclass.com/classes /steve-martin-teaches-comedy.

5. DETERMINING THE RIGHT MIND-SET

78 *B-corporation:* "Certified B Corporations," B Lab, accessed October 4, 2017, https://www.bcorporation.net/.
risk of slowing sales: "Seventh Generation Staffers Line Dry Their Laundry," *Seventh Generation,* Burlington, VT, July 1, 2010, https://www .seventhgeneration.com/nurture-nature/seventh-generation-staffers -line-dry-their-laundry.
$250 million in revenue: Beth Kowitt, "Seventh Generation CEO: Here's How the Unilever Deal Went Down," *Fortune,* September 20, 2016, http:// fortune.com/2016/09/20/seventh-generation-unilever-deal/.

79 *Branson summed up purpose:* Richard Branson, "5 Ways to Build a Project with Purpose," *Virgin,* July 16, 2014, https://www.virgin.com/richard -branson/5-ways-build-project-purpose.

81 *positive economic impacts for companies:* Michael E. Porter and Mark R. Kramer, "Strategy and Society: The Link Between Competitive Advantage and Corporate Social Responsibility," *Harvard Business Re-*

view, December 2006, https://hbr.org/2006/12/strategy-and-society
-the-link-between-competitive-advantage-and-corporate-social
-responsibility.

81 *at the University of Quebec:* Robert J. Vallerand, "On the Psychology of Passion: In Search of What Makes People's Lives Most Worth Living," January 2007, https://www.researchgate.net/publication/228347175_On_the
_Psychology_of_Passion_In_Search_of_What_Makes_People's_Lives
_Most_Worth_Living.

82 *following your passion is fundamentally flawed:* Cal Newport, *So Good They Can't Ignore You: Why Skills Trump Passion in the Quest for Work You Love* (New York: Grand Central Publishing, 2012), xviii.

   engaging work helps you develop passion: William MacAskill, *Doing Good Better: How Effective Altruism Can Help You Make a Difference* (New York: Avery, 2015), 147–178.

86 *not be just a job but an adventure:* Jeffrey Jensen Arnett and Elizabeth Fishel, "Is 30 the New 20 for Young Adults?" *AARP*, Washington, D.C., November 1, 2010, http://www.aarp.org/relationships/parenting/info
-10-2010/emerging_adulthood_thirtysomethings.html.

   always winners: M. P. Mueller, "How to Manage (and Avoid) Entitled Employees," *New York Times*, March 23, 2012, https://boss.blogs.nytimes
.com/2012/03/23/managing-and-avoiding-entitled-employees/.

88 *attempting to focus on more than one priority:* Mary Czerwinski, Eric Horvitz, and Susan Wilhite, "A Diary Study of Task Switching and Interruptions," Microsoft Research, Redmond, WA, January 1, 2004, http://
erichorvitz.com/taskdiary.pdf, 4–6.

   reduced by more than ten points: "'Infomania' Worse Than Marijuana," BBC News, April 22, 2005, http://news.bbc.co.uk/2/hi/uk_news/4471607.stm.

   for every interruption: Gloria Mark, Daniela Gudick, and Ulrich Klocke, "The Cost of Interrupted Work: More Speed and Stress," https://www.ics
.uci.edu/~gmark/chi08-mark.pdf.

91 *we make bad decisions:* Cara Feinberg, "The Science of Scarcity: A Behavioral Economist's Fresh Perspectives on Poverty," *Harvard Magazine*, May/June 2015, https://www.harvardmagazine.com/2015/05/the
-science-of-scarcity.

92 *fifty-five hours a week:* John Pencavel, "The Productivity of Work Hours," IZA Discussion Paper 8129, Institute for the Study of Labor, Bonn, Germany, April 2014, http://ftp.iza.org/dp8129.pdf, 52–54.

6. PERSONALITY MATTERS

97 *lose 17,000 followers within hours:* Anthony H. Normore, *Handbook of Research on Effective Communication, Leadership, and Conflict Resolution* (Hershey, PA: IGI Global, 2016), 151–153.

wander 46.9 percent of the time: Matthew A. Killingsworth and Daniel T. Gilbert, "A Wandering Mind Is an Unhappy Mind," *Science* 330, no. 6006 (November 12, 2010): 932, http://science.sciencemag.org/content/330 /6006/932.long.

100 *ignore everyone else*: Evan Carmichael, "Guy Kawasaki's Top 10 Rules for Success (@GuyKawasaki)," YouTube, posted March 14, 2016, https:// www.youtube.com/watch?v=nYv4W2IUNso.

101 *hire journalists to denigrate*: Sam Thielman and Dominic Rushe, "Government-Backed Egg Lobby Tried to Crack Food Startup, Emails Show," *Guardian*, September 2, 2015, https://www.theguardian.com/us-news /2015/sep/02/usda-american-egg-board-hampton-creek-just-mayo.

"Can we pool our money to put a hit on him?": Deena Shanker, "There Is Literally a U.S. Government Conspiracy Against Vegan Mayo," *Quartz*, September 2, 2015, https://qz.com/493958/there-is-literally-a-us-government -conspiracy-against-vegan-mayo/.

7. THE ONE CUSTOMER

106 *great customer service*: "2011 Customer Experience Impact Report: Getting to the Heart of the Consumer and Brand Relationship," *Oracle*, Redwood Shores, CA, 2012, http://www.oracle.com/us/products/applications/cust -exp-impact-report-epss-1560493.pdf.

ten times as much as their first purchase: The original study is out of print. However, "Increasing Customer Satisfaction," a summary of the 1974– 1979 study and the 1984–1986 studies for the U.S. Office of Consumer Affairs, was published by the U.S. Consumer Information Center, Pueblo, CO, 1986

don't ever return: Ruby Newell-Legner, "Understanding Our Customers and Their Loyalty" (video), Seven Star Service, Littleton, CO, 2014, http:// www.7starservice.com/products/secrets-to-keeping-our-customers -happy/video.

108 *less on the tangibles of a product*: Marc Beaujean, Jonathan Davidson, and Stacey Madge, "The 'Moment of Truth' in Customer Service," *McKinsey Quarterly* (February 2006), http://www.mckinsey.com /business-functions/organization/our-insights/the-moment-of-truth -in-customer-service.

109 *word-of-mouth referrals*: Anita Campbell, "November 2005 Survey 'Selling to Small Business'" (letter from the publisher), *Small Business Trends*, November 2005, https://smallbiztrends.com/wp-content/uploads/2008 /11/sellingtosmbiznovember.pdf.

110 *help your business*: "The Business Case for Loving Customers," *HelpScout*, accessed June 23, 2017, https://www.helpscout.net/whole-company -support/.

111 *"empathy index"*: Belinda Parmar, "The Most (and Least) Empathetic Companies," *Harvard Business Review,* November 27, 2015, https://hbr.org/2015/11/2015-empathy-index.

112 *internally led innovations:* Gary L. Lilien, Pamela D. Morrison, Kathleen Searls, Mary Sonnack, and Eric von Hippel, "Performance Assessment of the Lead User Idea Generation Process for New Product Development," April 1, 2002, https://evhippel.files.wordpress.com/2013/08/morrison-et-al-2002.pdf.

115 *number-one most innovative company:* Jeff Kauflin, "The World's Most Innovative Growth Companies: 2017," *Forbes,* May 17, 2017, https://www.forbes.com/innovative-companies/list/.

34 percent increase in sales revenue: "SalesForce Pardot Customer Success," SalesForce Pardot, accessed October 4, 2017, https://www.pardot.com/why-pardot/customer-success.

119 *far less for malpractice:* Aaron E. Carroll, "To Be Sued Less, Doctors Should Consider Talking to Patients More," *New York Times,* June 1, 2015, https://www.nytimes.com/2015/06/02/upshot/to-be-sued-less-doctors-should-talk-to-patients-more.html.

malpractice filings dropped by half: Kevin Sack, "Doctors Say 'I'm Sorry' Before 'See You in Court,'" *New York Times,* May 18, 2008, http://www.nytimes.com/2008/05/18/us/18apology.html.

in most cases apologizing: University of Nottingham, "Saying Sorry Really Does Cost Nothing," *ScienceDaily,* September 23, 2009, www.sciencedaily.com/releases/2009/09/090923105815.htm.

120 *one of the ten most-hated companies in America:* Douglas A. McIntyre, "The 10 Most Hated Companies in America," *24/7WallSt,* January 13, 2012, http://247wallst.com/special-report/2012/01/13/the-10-most-hated-companies-in-america/3/.

didn't answer support requests on social media: Anna Drennan, "Consumer Study: 88% Less Likely to Buy from Companies Who Ignore Complaints in Social Media," *Conversocial,* December 19, 2011, http://www.conversocial.com/blog/consumer-study-88-less-likely-to-buy-from-companies-who-ignore-complaints-in-social-media.

121 *don't align with their actions:* Luigi Guiso, Paola Sapienza, and Luigi Zingales, "The Value of Corporate Culture," September 2013, http://economics.mit.edu/files/9721.

"commitment drift": Maryam Kouchaki, Elizabeth Doty, and Francesca Gino, "Does Your Company Keep Its Promises? Revealing and Addressing Commitment Drift in Business," Harvard University, Edmond J. Safra Center for Ethics, July 21, 2014, https://ethics.harvard.edu/blog/does-your-company-keep-its-promises-revealing-and-addressing-commitment-drift.

8. SCALABLE SYSTEMS

127 *low salaries, and unfair treatment:* Naomi Klein, *No Is Not Enough: Resisting Trump's Shock Politics and Winning the World We Need* (New York: Haymarket Books, 2017), 113.

129 *return on investment of 3,800 percent:* Jordie van Rijn, "National Client Email Report 2015," *Data & Marketing Association,* 2015, https://dma.org .uk/uploads/ckeditor/National-client-email-2015.pdf.

130 *26 percent more likely to be opened:* Campaign Monitor, "The New Rules of Email Marketing," https://www.campaignmonitor.com/resources /guides/email-marketing-new-rules/.

   segmented automation emails: "Q1 2017 Email Trends and Benchmarks Show Increase in Desktop Open Rates," *Epsilon,* July 24, 2017, http:// pressroom.epsilon.com/q1-2017-north-america-email-trends-and -benchmarks-show-increase-in-desktop-open-rates-2/, 7, 11.

9. TEACH EVERYTHING YOU KNOW

142 *1,200 clients of an investment firm:* Andreas B. Eisingerich and Simon J. Bell, "Customer Education Increases Trust," *MIT Sloan Management Review,* October 1, 2008, https://sloanreview.mit.edu/article/customer -education-increases-trust/.

145 *advice from experts:* Brandon Keim, "Given 'Expert' Advice, Brains Shut Down," *Wired,* March 25, 2009, https://www.wired.com/2009/03 /financebrain/.

10. PROPERLY UTILIZING TRUST AND SCALE

152 *92 percent of consumers:* Cited in "Consumer Trust in Online, Social and Mobile Advertising Grows," *Nielsen,* April 10, 2012, http://www.nielsen .com/ca/en/insights/news/2012/consumer-trust-in-online-social-and -mobile-advertising-grows.html.

   rated referrals: Anita Campbell, "85 Percent of Small Businesses Get Customers Through Word of Mouth," *Small Business Trends,* June 10, 2015, https://smallbiztrends.com/2014/06/small-businesses-get-customers -through-word-of-mouth.html.

153 *smaller businesses thrive:* Fareena Sultan and William Qualls, "Placing Trust at the Center of Your Internet Strategy," *MIT Sloan Management Review* 42, no. 1 (Fall 2000): 39–48.

   only 29 percent actually do so: "Anatomy of the Referral: Economics of Loyalty," Texas Tech University, Lubbock, TX, and Advisor Impact, Salisbury, NC, December 2010.

   88 percent of American consumers: "Local Consumer Review Survey 2014," *BrightLocal,* 2014, https://www.brightlocal.com/learn/local-consumer -review-survey-2014/.

11. LAUNCHING AND ITERATING IN TINY STEPS

168 *predictability, accessibility:* George Whitesides, "Towards a Science of Simplicity," TED Talks, February 2010, https://www.ted.com/talks /george_whitesides_toward_a_science_of_simplicity.

170 *the most-funded KickStarter project ever:* "Pebble Time — Awesome Smartwatch, No Compromises," *Kickstarter,* accessed October 9, 2017, https://www.kickstarter.com/projects/getpebble/pebble-time-awesome -smartwatch-no-compromises.

(didn't ensure Pebble's long-term success): Lauren Goode, "Fitbit Bought Pebble for Much Less Than Originally Reported," *The Verge,* February 22, 2017, https://www.theverge.com/2017/2/22/14703108/fitbit-bought -pebble-for-23-millionw.

171 *best suited for consumer-facing products:* Olav Sorenson, "Could Crowd-funding Reshape Entrepreneurship?" *Yale Insights,* July 14, 2016, http://insights.som.yale.edu/insights/could-crowdfunding-reshape -entrepreneurship.

who are predominantly white males: Gené Teare and Ned Desmond, "The First Comprehensive Study on Women in Venture Capital and Their Impact on Female Founders," *TechCrunch,* April 19, 2016, https://techcrunch .com/2016/04/19/the-first-comprehensive-study-on-women-in-venture -capital/.

other white men: Alison Wood Brooks, Laura Huang, Sarah Wood Kearney, and Fiona E. Murray, "Investors Prefer Entrepreneurial Ventures Pitched by Attractive Men," *PNAS,* February 20, 2014, http://www.hbs .edu/faculty/Publication%20Files/Brooks%20Huang%20Kearney%20 Murray_59b551a9-8218-4b84-be15-eaff58009767.pdf; see also Malin Malmström, Jeaneth Johansson, and Joakim Wincent, "Gender Stereotypes and Venture Support Decisions: How Governmental Venture Capitalists Socially Construct Entrepreneurs' Potential," Entrepreneurship: Theory and Practice 41, no. 5 (September 2017): 833–860.

hitting their fundraising goals than men: "Women Unbound: Unleashing Female Entrepreneurial Potential," PwC and the Crowdfunding Center, July 2017, https://www.pwc.com/gx/en/diversity-inclusion/assets /women-unbound.pdf.

175 *you've launched too late:* Anthony Ha, "LinkedIn Founder Reid Hoffman's 10 Rules of Entrepreneurship," *VentureBeat,* March 15, 2011, https://venturebeat.com/2011/03/15/reid-hoffman-10-rules-of -entrepreneurship/.

simply good enough to launch: Jim Collins, *"Good to Great," Fast Company,* October 2001, http://www.jimcollins.com/article_topics/articles/good -to-great.html.

176 *"Every company now is a technology company":* Anil Dash, "There Is No

'Technology Industry,'" *Medium,* August 19, 2016, https://medium.com/humane-tech/there-is-no-technology-industry-44774dfb3ed7.

177 *"are even on the radar screen in terms of competition":* Rick Munarriz, "Blockbuster CEO Has Answers," *Motley Fool,* December 10, 2008, https://www.fool.com/investing/general/2008/12/10/blockbuster-ceo-has-answers.aspx.

"Screw the Nano": Clint Ecker, "Motorola: 'Screw the Nano!'" *Ars Technica,* September 23, 2005, https://arstechnica.com/gadgets/2005/09/1352/.

"staring at a plywood box every night": "Worst Tech Predictions of All Time," *Telegraph,* June 29, 2016, http://www.telegraph.co.uk/technology/0/worst-tech-predictions-of-all-time/darryl-zanuck-in-1964/.

12. THE HIDDEN VALUE OF RELATIONSHIPS

183 *social networking section of Apple's app store:* Sarah Perez, "Video Texting App Glide Is Going 'Viral,' Now Ranked Just Ahead of Instagram in App Store," *TechCrunch,* July 24, 2013, https://techcrunch.com/2013/07/24/video-texting-app-glide-is-going-viral-now-ranked-just-ahead-of-instagram-in-app-store/.

184 *great customer experience:* Sarah Perez, "When Growth Hacking Goes Bad," *TechCrunch,* January 3, 2014, https://techcrunch.com/2014/01/03/when-growth-hacking-goes-bad/.

path to failure, exponentially: Andy Johns, "What Does Andy Johns Think of Pinterest's Rapid Growth? What Factors Do You Believe Drove Its Viral Growth, Especially from 2011–Present?" *Quora,* March 17, 2014, https://www.quora.com/Andy-Johns-4/What-does-Andy-Johns-think-of-Pinterests-rapid-growth-What-factors-do-you-believe-drove-its-viral-growth-especially-from-2011-present/answer/Andy-Johns?share=1&srid=hiM.

for attention at any time: Des Traynor, "If It's Important, Don't Hack It," *Inside Intercom,* February 12, 2013, https://blog.intercom.com/if-its-important-dont-hack-it/.

185 *rate of repayment on Kiva is 97 percent:* See the Kiva website at https://www.kiva.org/about (accessed October 13, 2017).

187 *coining the term in 1916:* "L. J. Hanifan," *Wikipedia,* last modified June 2, 2017, https://en.wikipedia.org/wiki/L._J._Hanifan.

189 *comes from the social capital of a business:* Willy Bolander, Cinthia B. Satornino, Douglas E. Hughes, and Gerald R. Ferris, "Social Networks Within Sales Organizations: Their Development and Importance for Salesperson Performance," *American Marketing Association,* 2015, https://www.ama.org/publications/JournalOfMarketing/Pages/social-networks-sales-salesperson-performance.aspx.

190 *several courses and workshops on the subject:* "Customer Relationship

Strategies: The Key to Developing Long-Term Customer Relationships," McGill University, School of Continuing Studies, accessed October 12, 2017, https://www.mcgill.ca/continuingstudies/programs-and-courses /business-and-management/courses-and-workshops/cementing.

191 *bottom part of the pyramid:* "The Social Brain and Its Superpowers: Matthew Lieberman, PhD, at TEDxStLouis," filmed September 19, 2013, YouTube, posted October 7, 2013, https://www.youtube.com /watch?v=NNhk3owF7RQ.

not harming animals: "Compliance with Appropriate Implementation of Animal Experiments in Research and Development Activities at Otsuka Group Companies," Otsuka Holdings Co., Ltd., accessed October 13, 2017, https://www.otsuka.com/en/rd/compliance/.

192 *caused loyal and long-term customers to revolt:* "Keep Daiya Vegan! Reject the Otsuka Acquisition," Change.org, accessed October 13, 2017, https:// www.change.org/p/daiya-canada-keep-daiya-vegan-reject-the-otsuka -acquisition.

193 *loyal stake in your business:* Jim Dougherty, "5 Steps to Building Great Business Relationships," *Harvard Business Review,* December 5, 2014, https:// hbr.org/2014/12/5-steps-to-building-great-business-relationships.

194 *dimension of their business:* "Capitalizing on Complexity: Insights from the IBM Global CEO Study 2010," IBM Corporation, 2010, http://www-07 .ibm.com/events/my/ceoworkshop/downloads/1.pdf.

13. STARTING A COMPANY OF ONE — MY STORY

201 *"People want to be the noun":* Austin Kleon, "The Noun and the Verb," July 22, 2015, https://austinkleon.com/2015/07/22/the-noun-and-the-verb/.

Index

About the author

Beginning as a corporate web designer and internet consultant, Paul Jarvis first spent years working with top professional athletes like Warren Sapp, Steve Nash, and Shaquille O'Neal with their online presence, and with large companies like Yahoo, Microsoft, Mercedes-Benz and Warner Music. He then migrated to working with online entrepreneurs like Marie Forleo, Danielle LaPorte, and Kris Carr to help build their online brands.

These days, Paul Jarvis spends his time writing, creating software, podcasting, and teaching online courses with his own company of one which is called Mighty Small Ventures. His writing and ideas have been featured around the internet in places like *WIRED*, *Fast Company*, *USA Today*, *VICE News*, and by MailChimp and Adobe.

When not working, Paul enjoys gardening, driving fast cars, sarcasm and hiking. He lives on an island off the coast of British Columbia with his wife Lisa.

Paul writes a weekly newsletter called *The Sunday Dispatches*, where he shares his latest writing and ideas. It's free and you can sign up at www.pjrvs.com/signup/. You can also find him on Twitter @pjrvs.

To learn more about how to start your own company of one, join the Co1 community, listen to the Companies of One podcast, and get other free resources related to the book, visit the website: www.ofone.co.

9288